MW00681389

CACHE THE CZECH
A Divine Journey To America

Father Walter Marek

SMD Books
Traverse City, Michigan

Cache The Czech: A Divine Journey To America

SMD Books
smdbooks@excite.com

Copyright 2007 by Walter Marek & Kyle A. Hamilton
All Right Reserved

ISBN-13: 978-0-9798432-0-4
ISBN-10: 0-9798432-0-0

Cover Design: Kyle A. Hamilton
Compiled & Edited: Kyle A. Hamilton

Printed By Signature Book Printing
www.sbpbooks.com

CONTENTS

Coffee Grinders, Clutches & Columbus • Childhood Impressions of
Jewish People • The Rocek Family • The Roceks & The Nazi Camp at
Terezin • The Kaplans & The Great Shoe Order • The Gymnasium &
Origins of anti-Semitism • Czech Faith • Pre & Post War Czech Political
Parties • German Dissent in Sudetenland • Vacation to Sudetenland 1931
• The COD Automobile

Seminary Life & Sudeten German Seminarians • The Munich Pact (1938)
• The Nazis Take Czechoslovakia • How The Nazis Identified Jews • As-
sassination of Heydrich and Nazi Reprisal • Without Proper Identification
• Popular Savings & The Lidice Massacre • Nazi Siege of a Town Near
Turnov • Nazi Occupation & My Arrival in Litomysl • Nazis Force Czechs
into Labor • My Forced Labor Draft • Hitler's Plan for Czechs • The Czech
Resistance Trained in England • Czech Resistance by Russian Partisans •
My Vow of Non-Violence • The Provostship

The Prague Uprising • Tensions in Litomysl • The Communist Revolution
• The Czech Underground • Underground Operations • Failed Uprisings •
The Surfacing Underground • Escape Warning

Abducted by The Communists • Escape from Litomyšl • Escape to German in 1949 • Refugee Without ID • Interrogation • Bishop Doepfner of
Wurzburg • Eichstätt, Germany • The Aftermath of My Escape

CONTENTS

ACKNOWLDGEMENTS

My thanks go to the three people, who showed great patience with me as I wrote this book of my memories. First of all, to our Most Reverend Bishop, Patrick G. Cooney of Gaylord, Michigan, who is endorsing this book.

To my friend, Mrs. Matie "Muggs" Richards, who helped me greatly, after I was stricken by the Parkinson's disease.

To my editor, Mr. Kyle Hamilton who deserves all the credit for this book. He worked on it for several months, pasting together a collection of e-mail messages I'd written, then preparing the manuscript for printing.

Several friends of mine, who read this book, were very excited and told me that they will recommend it to others.

In this book, you will read about events as I saw them or as I read of them or heard of them from friends or acquittances. Every statement in this book is true. It happened as it is written.

Father Walter Marek
Traverse City, Michigan 2007

FORWARD

I am profoundly grateful for your series of articles about the Jewish questions in Czechoslovakia. Your recollections are a great gift not only for me, but also for many others with whom I will share them.

I have visited the Jewish quarter in Prague, of course, and know that Hitler wished it be protected "as a memorial to an extinct race." One of my regrets is that I didn't visit Terezin, about which I know a great deal from my studies of history. When I stayed in Poprad (Slovakia) as guests of the Zachar family this summer, I was keenly aware that the horrible camp at Auschwitz was a mere 75 miles to our north.

When I taught in Vienna in 1999, history Professor Karl Vocelka of the University of Vienna traveled with me, our guests and about 30 students to the Malthausen concentration camp near Linz. While I knew of these dreadful camps through reading history, I'd never experienced them first-hand or "viscerally," and the experience was shocking, felt in the stomach as though I'd been hit. I could not understand how a culture that produced Beethoven, Goethe, and so many other great minds, could also produce such intentional savagery and humiliation on a massive scale never even imagined in human history. Not only Jews, but "liberal" professors, gay people and anyone considered (by Nazis of course) as undesirables were "eliminated" (i.e. murdered). To this day I cannot come to terms with it, even though I have many fine Australian friends with whom I've discussed this. (To the great credit of my students, they examined the camp without a single word exchanged between them for a full 90 minutes!)

This was a time of incredible brutality. Thank you for exchanging your first-hand recollections. I was born in 1942 – my father saw no military action but worked in a war munitions factory. One of my earliest memories is of driving to downtown Grand Rapids to hear the ringing of the bells on V-E Day. Many of my uncles served in the European or Pacific theaters (what a strange word for killing) and all returned alive.

Douglas J. Scripps, Professor Emeritus of Music. A.B., Calvin College; M.M., University of Michigan. 1985-2002. October 2005.

INTRODUCTION

Many people have asked me to write about my life experiences. Mainly, they have asked me to answer four questions: (1) How did the Czechoslovakian people feel about Jews? (2) Did the Czechoslovakians try to help Jews during World War II? (3) What was your life like during the war? (4) How did you come to the United States?

These are wonderful questions and I feel honored that anyone would be interested at all. I know a great many things about pre and post-war Europe, but I shall not write about Poland or Germany or Hungary or other countries. I shall write only about my own country, Czechoslovakia. My goal in this work is to answer the questions above by describing my personal experiences.

Today, I am a naturalized American citizen, but my life and the history of Czechoslovakia are intertwined. I was born in Prague on Sunday, September 29, 1918, one month before the first Republic of Czechoslovakia was established. Therefore, it is true to say that I was born in the capital of Bohemia, then part of the Austro-Hungarian Empire. I came into this world on the same day that Bulgaria became the first European country to sign an armistice, marking the end of World War I.

I have lived history in a way that gives me unique insight. Certainly, by 2006 few of my contemporaries remain alive to speak of those dangerous times. I shall begin this story with childhood memories, then bring you into my life as a student in Prague, a Catholic seminarian, a Catholic priest and a humble man falling into the arms of America after World War II. Of course, there is much to tell, but even more that shall never be told. This is my story. Please enjoy.

Father Walter Marek 2007

CHAPTER 1

THE SPRINGTIME OF YOUTH

I grew up in Horní Jelení, Czechoslovakia. Horní Jelení means "Upper Elk Country" and in my youth it was a town of just 2,000 people. Everything that can happen happened in Horní Jelení, both good and bad. I would like to talk first about the bad and be done with it, but my memories are complex interlocking pieces that cannot be separated.

COFFEE GRINDERS, CLUTCHES & COLUMBUS

Coffee was roasted several times a week at three general stores in Horní Jelení - Kopriva, Schejbal and Prudic. Each store had a stove wherein the beans where roasted with great care. When I close my eyes, I can still smell the heavenly aroma of roasting coffee beans and see the streets of our little town. Not everyone could afford good coffee. Many made their own from roasted wheat and chicory. Chicory was grown on many local farms and sold to large companies like Balounek.

I sometimes wonder what happened to such companies during the Communist occupation, when almost all company owners were banished from their businesses, imprisoned or killed. Those who joined the Communist Party were lucky just to stay alive and have menial work. It would be impossible for young people today to understand what the imposition of Communist rule in Czechoslovakia was like. After February 1948, business owners were simply informed that they no longer owned their businesses. They could go home or be arrested. Please forgive me, as I'm getting well ahead of myself.

Today, good coffee remains a true privilege for me and a way to revisit my memories. When I was a boy, my grandmother had a coffee clutch every afternoon at 4 o'clock with her friend Mrs.

Kapounova. Mrs. Kapounova was originally from Prague and had attended many operas there as a young lady. Just the smell of coffee often returns me to her stories of going to the finest theatres of Prague in a horse-drawn carriage. She was always delighted when I played music from her favorite operas on my violin.

Me at age 7

My family preferred Schejbal's roasted coffee, but my father was a good friend of Mr. Kopriva. He was an honest businessman and the chairman of our Fire Department. My father sent me to his store every year to buy tickets for the Fireman's Ball. Of course, the Prudic's claimed that their coffee was the very best in town. Their son Lada was an excellent violinist. He had a group that played local dances and I often sat in on piano. The percussionist from that group was Rudy Rocen and he is alive and well today, a young 95 years of age.

Horní Jelení had three common surnames: Janeba, Kaplan and Marek. Many Janebas and Kaplans had the same first name, so we gave them comical nicknames. There was "In the corner" Janeba, "Tarzan" Janeba (because he was a great wrestler), "Violinmaker" Janeba, etc. Two people in town were named "Karel Marek," so my father distinguished himself by using his middle initial (Karel B. Marek). The "B" was for Bedrich. I recall one Kaplan whose nickname was "Baron." Baron Kaplan owned a coffee grinder factory right behind our house. The factory featured an impossibly tall brick chimney. There was a famous saying in Horní Jelení, "When Columbus arrived in America, two men from Horní Jelení were waiting to sell him a coffee grinder!" Apparently, Columbus had bought several Kaplan grinders. When Baron Kaplan got old he sold his factory. My father and a neighbor each purchased half of the building. We got the half with the chimney. After some debate, the chimney was taken down one brick at a time, yielding over 20,000 individual bricks. Our family scrubbed and cleaned each brick and used them to build an addition and garage on the back of our house. We left nothing to waste.

My mother taught sewing to local girls. I am in the front.

CHILDHOOD IMPRESSIONS OF JEWISH PEOPLE

My family owned a textile store and sewing business in Horní Jelení for many years. In the 1920's, business in the new Republic of Czechoslovakia was very good and my Father dreamed of building his own textile factory to manufacture fabrics, sweaters and other garments.

In those days, the Czechoslovakian textile industry was mainly in the hands of Jews. My family knew a number of textile wholesalers and traveling salesmen who were Jewish. As a young boy, I learned that Jews have their own religion and synagogues. When I was old enough to accompany my father on business, I met the Bermans Brothers.

The Bermans were successful Jewish wholesale textile merchants. I admired the way they handled fabrics and sold their goods. Perhaps my memory of them is especially fond because they always treated me with ice cream! Whenever I arrived at the store, Mr. Bermans sent a clerk to get me a dish of ice cream. Even as a child, it was obvious to me that these Jewish people had a gift for conducting business.

As far as I know, Horní Jelení never had a sizeable Jewish population or a Synagogue. My grandmother could recall only one Jewish family that had lived in town. She told me that they had operated a tiny store on a side street. Some 80 years later, a great coincidence would connect me to that very family.

THE ROCEK FAMILY

Horní Jelení has a very nice recreation area called "Radost," which means "Pleasure" in Czech. Radost was built by the Communists to keep young Czechs gathered in what were called "Pioneer Groups." Pioneer Groups were actually Communist organizations designed to immerse young Czechs in Communist propaganda and gather information on underground dissent. In 1997, I founded in this area *The*

Czech Music Camp for Youth, which emulates Interlochen and Blue Lake Fine Arts Camp in Michigan.

Over the past 10 years, about 70 American students have traveled to The Czech Republic to attend my music camp. Two of these American students were Julian and Laura Rocek. Their Jewish grandparents, Eva & Jan Rocek brought them to the camp. I learned that Eva & Jan were holocaust survivors originally from Czechoslovakia. Their story is one of great courage and redemption.

The first time Eva Rocek visited my music camp, she did not know that she had roots in Horní Jelení. Some months later, while tracing her family ancestry, Eva learned that her grandmother had lived in Horní Jelení and was from the family my Grandmother recalled. This gave me a strong feeling of connection to the Roceks.

THE ROCEKS & THE NAZI CAMP AT TEREZIN

Now in their 80's, Eva & Jan Rocek met as teenagers while imprisoned in the Nazi concentration camp at Terezin. Terezin was a lovely city in Sudetenland, which the Nazis converted into a "Model" concentration camp very early in the war. The Nazis wanted to show the Red Cross an "ideal" concentration camp where music, theatre and opera were encouraged. For a time, Eva Rocek even sang in the camp choir at Terezin. Of course, the hidden parts of Terezin were like any other Nazi concentration camp. One of my fellow seminarians and a professor from the seminary were tortured and died at the camp.

My classmate died there on the very last day of the war. The professor, who was also our spiritual director in the seminary, died there some weeks earlier. He was beaten to death by a Nazi guard who spoke the Czech language. Someone near the camp witnessed the beating and the event was described in our local newspaper. The article was very graphic; recounting the last horrible moments of the priest's life who pleaded with the guard, "For God's sake mister

5

have mercy." The guard was possessed with brutality and seemed to take pleasure in beating the helpless priest. He was beaten repeatedly on the abdomen with fists and clubs until he died, probably of internal injuries and bleeding.

Eva & Jan were eventually transferred to Auschwitz and somehow managed to survive until the camp was liberated. They married and both became professors of chemistry in Prague. During the "Prague Spring" in 1968, they took a vacation with their two young sons to East Germany where by chance they found a tourist boat going to Denmark and freedom. They were very lucky that sympathetic Danes helped them stay in the country. From Denmark they traveled to England and finally on to Chicago.

Eva & Jan started a new life in Chicago as chemistry professors at the University of Chicago. Their sons have also become professors in America. It is an honor to know the Rocek family and their story of redemption.

Jewish influence in Horní Jelení was not noticeable during my childhood. One local man by the name of Isaac was rumored to have Jewish ancestry, but we all knew him to be a Catholic. After Eva Rocek's ancestor's left town, there was only one person of Jewish ancestry living in Horní Jelení, Mrs. Kaplan.

THE KAPLANS & THE GREAT SHOE ORDER

During my teenage years, when I came home from school in Prague, I spent a lot of time with Josef Kaplan. Joseph's mother was Jewish. His father was famous for saving our town during the depression, which in Czech was called the "Krise" meaning "Crises." This is a wonderful little story.

Along with fresh roasted coffee, the citizens of Horní Jelení had shoemaking in their blood. It was often said, "On one side of every street in Horní Jelení there is a shoemaker in every second house. On the other side of that street there is a shoe-maker in every house!" Around 1929, probably through the influence of his wife,

Mr. Kaplan traveled to the United States and obtained a huge order for Czech-made shoes. Making the shoes to fill this order kept many local families afloat during the depression. My father was proud of Mr. Kaplan and later expressed regret that he'd declined his offer to form a partnership in 1920.

During the depression our textile business faltered and my father decided to diversify. He started a small bank in Horní Jelení called *Popular Savings*. I was a teenager by then and able to help him with the new enterprise. *Popular Savings* became my introduction to the principles of finance, which is a valuable education for any young man. I was to learn much more about business and finance in the seminary. A fellow seminarian with 4 years of advanced business education took the time to teach me many things. My knowledge of finance, accounting and statistics would serve me very well in the years to come.

THE GYMNASIUM & ORIGINS OF ANTI-SEMITISM

From age 11 to 18 (1929 to 1937), I attended the Arch Diocesan's Gymnasium in Prague. The Gymnasium was a boarding school for boys run by the Jesuits. Some 350 boys in 8 different classes attended the school. Two hundred and fifty of us lived at the school; another 100 came from around Prague and were known as Externists. I believe the Jesuits provided us with the finest education in Czechoslovakia and perhaps in all of Europe. I regret to admit however, that our education was slanted against Jews. It is very difficult for me to write about this fact now. Even at this moment I must pause and collect myself.

One must consider the circumstances of the school. The Gymnasium occupied a large piece of property in an affluent section of Prague and was surrounded by beautiful villas owned by rich Jewish families. This fact must have caused some friction between the Jesuits and neighboring Jews. As young students, we had only one criterion for neighboring Jewish families. When we accidentally kicked our ball onto the property of a Jew, most were understanding and returned it without issue. Others returned the ball only after we promised to never, ever play near their home again. You can guess who we liked better!

Adjacent to the Gymnasium we observed the building of a particularly luxurious villa, which would be the home of a rich Jewish family by the name of Petchek. The Petchek family owned a large bank, which frequently loaned money to the Czechoslovakian government to cover payroll shortages. I heard later that when the Nazis took Prague, the Petchek family was secretly given access to a train, allowing them to escape the country. This neighborhood was also home to the famous violinist Kubelik and his son Rafael. Rafael became a distinguished symphony orchestra conductor, working in Prague, Munich and Chicago.

My education at the Gymnasium had an undercurrent of anti-Semitism. The school library contained works by Jules Verne, as well as many popular and traditional authors. It also contained a series of anti-Semitic books written by a Catholic priest named Kosmak. Kosmak's stories often portrayed Jews as rich from corruption and morally bankrupt.

During my time as a student, the Gymnasium condoned anti-Semitism. What I remember with some horror today is a play we performed every year. It was a very large production, performed in our auditorium with a full orchestra. The central character was a poor, depraved Jewish man. I can still hear one of the accompanying songs in my mind. The lyrics went something like this:

There was a Jewish man,
and he was like the hunchback of Notre Dame,
and he had very big nose, nose, nose,
and he had a big nose.

Further verses I care not to remember. On stage an actor portrayed the man while another actor sang the song. This sketch always brought great applause from the audience. I remember that

I never felt good about the applause, even when I was playing in the orchestra. How was it possible, such humiliation of a poor, old, sick man portrayed on the stage as entertainment? How could my teachers condone such a play? That program and these questions still haunt me today.

In my memory, Czechs were generally not friendly to Jews. I believe this was simply because most Jews were successful in their professions and had money. Jewish culture includes systems of producing and perpetuating family wealth. Czech rancor was especially palpable in Prague's medical community, which boasted some very distinguished Jewish doctors.

I recall one Jewish doctor with the surname Levi, whose wife I met during the war. She was a soprano and I sometimes accompanied her on piano or organ. She spoke openly about the strong anti-Semitic currents in Prague. Doctor Levi managed to escape before the Nazis invaded and found work as a ship's doctor for the Allies.

Gymnasium Orchestra 1929. I am in the third row, sixth from left.

Gymnasium Class 1933. I am in front row, 4th from left.

CZECH FAITH

During my lifetime, the country now called the Czech Republic has undergone eight name changes and as many political and economic upheavals. From the end of the Austro-Hungarian Empire in 1918, through the Nazi occupation (1938-1945) and through the Communist occupation (1948-1989), my country and my people have known little but change. Sometimes political changes have included changes in state policies on religion. Through it all, faith has remained a constant for the Czech people. Faith differs from politics and economics. Faith resides in the human heart and can sustain a heart through many outside changes. This is one of the reasons I decided to attend the seminary and become a Catholic priest.

During the Austro-Hungarian Empire, Catholicism was the official national religion. Therefore, all public and government positions required membership to the Catholic Church and included faith-based responsibilities. For instance, if you were a music teach-

10

er, then you had to play the organ at your local Catholic church. Many professionals were duty-bound in some way to the Catholic Church. The Austro-Hungarian Empire collapsed in October 1918 and Czechoslovakia was established as a model of democracy in Europe. Tomáš Masaryk became the first President of Czechoslovakia. Soon after taking office he proclaimed, "Catholics will have as many rights as they can secure for themselves." In response, more than one thousand Czech Catholic priests petitioned the Vatican for permission to get married and use only the Czech language in Mass and Liturgy. Naturally, Rome denied both petitions. Undeterred, many of these priests banded together and organized the Hussite National Church. Other Catholic priests chose to change professions and took positions in the new government, which was then gathering intelligent, educated and well-connected community leaders.

It was a special experience to meet one of these former priests. On one occasion, while visiting a Ministry of State building in Prague, I had a conversation with the Assistant Secretary. He was about 60 years old, good looking and possessed a wonderful personality. He studied me very closely during our conversation, which made me feel a little nervous. At the end of our talk he said, "I have a former classmate in your town by the name of Sperl. Please say hello to him for me." When I later met Dr. Sperl, who was a veterinarian, he asked me, "Did you know that gentleman was one of the former Catholic priests?"

PRE & POST WAR CZECH POLITICAL PARTIES

Pre-War Czechoslovakia had four main political parties: The Communist Party, The Social Democratic Party, The National Socialist Party and The Popular Party. The Popular Party was and remains today the party of Catholics and for anyone who believes in the Ten Commandments. Before the war, about half of the Social Democrats were communists, but unlike Communist party members, they

11

wanted to accomplish leadership without violence. The National Socialists were strictly against the Catholic Church and wanted to have a state without religion and God.

Therefore, it was the job of the Popular Party to defend the Catholic Church and its teachings. The Popular Party was never big, but it was very influential. I believe this was because our members were deeply religious and willing to sacrifice much for their faith. In my youth, about 15% of Czechs were members of the Popular Party. Today, only about 5% belong to the Popular Party.

When I was about 8 years old, the National Socialists had a big picnic in Horní Jelení and invited a well-known, anti-Catholic senator to speak. Naturally, my father would never be seen at such an event, but was very interested in what the senator would say. He solved this problem by sending me to listen and report back. I felt strange standing on the matted grass among the throng of Social Democrats. The senator looked like Theodore Roosevelt, with a heavy gold pocket watch chain dangling from his vest.

The senator used all the National Socialist clichés of the day and finished his speech in a most dramatic fashion. He said, "Ladies and gentleman, I want to tell you what to do." The whole audience listened intently, hanging on his next word. "Go to Christ!" All the people looked at each other; they did not come to hear about Christ! He repeated, "Go close to Christ!" I could feel an air of disbelief in the crowd. Someone next to me asked, "What is he talking about?" After a long and suspenseful pause the senator declared, "Get very close to Christ and stay very far from Rome!" At this, the audience exploded in applause. I squeezed from the crowd and ran home to perform the speech for my Father. He was most impressed!

The National Socialists were to suffer greatly after the war, when they organized an unsuccessful underground campaign against the Communists. By the time of my escape, I heard that the National Socialist underground actually sought to cooperate with the Popular Party underground. The Communists quickly smashed both movements.

Soon after taking control of Czechoslovakia, the Communists sent a strong message to all insurgent movements by publicly hanging two high-profile women, Dr. Matilda Horakova and Frana Zeminova. They sentenced the leader of the Popular Party to 27 years in a Communist prison. I was sentenced in absentia to 25 years, but I'm getting ahead of myself again.

GERMAN DISSENT IN SUDETENLAND

Germans and Czechs had lived together in Bohemia, Moravia, and Silesia for centuries. As Germany's population grew, many German families sought a better life to the east and to some degree all over the world. It seems that Germans are very adaptable and can prosper almost anywhere. I remember reflecting on this in 1974, when my travels took me to Sri Lanka. On the way into town from the airport, I saw a large sign providing directions. I was surprised to see the sign was written in German.

However well intended, the coexistence of Germans and Czechs always seemed conflicted. During his teenage years, my father lived in Sudetenland with his German uncle and attended a trade school. On the way home from school, aggressive German boys often confronted him, screaming "Bohmischer Hund" (Czech Dog). He and other Czech boys answered, "Deutche Krise" (German Rat). Sometimes, vicious fights would ensue.

I lived in Sudetenland for one summer and have to admit that the Sudeten Germans had many legitimate complaints. It was very difficult for the Czech government to fulfill the needs and wishes of the German minority in Sudetenland. However, the question must be asked; did the Czechoslovakian government do enough? Czechoslovakia was a democracy, but Germans were the majority population in Sudetenland. The German majority strained Czech nationalism and created political conflicts of interest. If Sudeten Germans felt disenfranchised by the Czech government, then they were completely disgusted by a system that seemed to appoint only

13

Czechs to key government positions. The Germans responded to the situation by establishing their own newspapers, operas, clubs and other cultural organizations. I remember a family vacation to Sudetenland in 1931.

VACATION TO SUDETENLAND IN 1931

My father had two Sudeten German cousins who lived in Nimes. I met them only once, when we had a new car that could make the 200-mile trip. Traveling 200 miles by automobile in 1931 was quite a feat, notwithstanding my father's rather poor driving skills. He greatly enjoyed the trip, but my mother was not so happy. I think this was because my cousin Fritz was a hearty drinker, who insisted on taking us to noisy nightclubs, where my mother felt most uncomfortable.

I was now 13 years old and intent upon becoming a musician, so the jazz I heard in these nightclubs was very exciting. I remember seeing a bass saxophone for the first time. Its player was a short, bespectacled man who stood on a stool to reach the mouthpiece. The sax must have been 6 inches taller than he! Of course, there were many people dancing and drinking and singing. Ladies in summer dresses spun around and landed in the arms of men. The whole scene was very exciting to me.

My mother was happy that we had front row seats for the Passion Play, which was performed that year in Nimes. The history of the Passion Play began in the Bavarian village of Oberammergau in 1633. Then in the middle of the 30-Years-War and having suffered terribly from the plague, the Oberammergau villagers swore to perform a "Play of the Suffering, Death and Resurrection of The Lord Jesus Christ" every ten years. This beautiful tradition was adopted in Nimes, where every five years a play was performed. The Nimes play seemed religiously and artistically perfect. I would say that it could easily compete with the Oberammergau play.

THE COD AUTOMOBILE

Of course, not all was bad between Czechs and Germans. It was because of a German family that we had a new car to drive to Nimes. As I mentioned before, my father was always pining to own a textile factory. There was a large factory in a neighboring town owned by a German family called Groh. My father invested a great sum of money in this factory. Unfortunately, the depression was too much for the Grohs and they were forced to declare bankruptcy. My father ended-up losing some 500,000 Czech crowns, which was an enormous bundle of money.

The Groh family had two boys my age, Hans and Jospeh. Joseph often invited me and other boys to their home in the summertime. We'd play soccer on the beautifully manicured lawn and have lunch together. The boys had a French nanny who after the bankruptcy took them in at her apartment, so they could continue their studies. Here comes the part about the car. After declaring bankruptcy, Mr. Groh promised to pay my father back. As a first payment, he would give us a brand new automobile, which at the time cost about 35,000 crowns. We were all very excited when the car was delivered, only to learn that it had not been paid for! My father ended up paying for the car too!

My father never showed animosity toward the Groh family. When the Nazis occupied Czechoslovakia, they got their factory back and tried again to make it work. Hans was killed on the Eastern front. I heard a rumor that Joseph had been a Nazi SS Officer, but I do not know this for sure. After the war ended, I found Josef's address and wrote a letter to him. He never replied to me. Years later, I learned that he lived alone and only came into town to visit the graves of his parents. Some things are best left in the past.

CHAPTER 2

THE SHADOWS OF WAR

SEMINARY LIFE & SUDETEN GERMAN SEMINARIANS

Prior to the war, almost one quarter of Czechoslovakia's population was German. By the late 1930's, the changing mood of Germans living in Czechoslovakia could be felt among my fellow seminarians. When I entered the seminary in 1937, we had about 50 Sudeten Germens and 100 Czechs in five classes. The Germans had their own academic clubs and a gazebo in the gardens. The Czechs also maintained separate facilities. Our combined activities were choir and free time in the gym. Some of the Germans were excellent gymnasts. We all got along pretty well, but our nationalist divisions became increasingly apparent as 1938 unfolded.

In seminary politics, there were clear indications that the German seminarians were becoming restless. They quietly demonstrated their discontent with national affairs by wearing bright white sox, which clashed terribly with their black sutans. On one occasion, the Germans demanded an audience with the Bishop and he attended several closed meetings with them. We heard later that they had asked for special treatment and had been disrespectful to the Bishop. Naturally, he did not give in to their demands. Things went on as before.

Seminary professors always lectured to us in Latin. They reviewed their lectures in Czech on Mondays and Thursdays, and in German on Tuesdays and Fridays. German seminarians had to practice their sermons in Czech and give a full sermon in Czech at the end of the year. Similarly, we Czechs were obliged to practice their sermons in German. Changing languages was always easier for us than for the Germans. Some of the German boys created hilarious scenes when they mispronounced difficult Czech words during their sermons. All the German seminarians finished the 1938 school year.

Some went on to become priests and others went into the German army. I was close to several of these boys and know of three that died in the war. They remain forever in my memory as smiling, intelligent boys who never experienced their 25th birthdays.

Me at age 20, outside the seminary.

THE MUNICH PACT (1938)

Hitler saw the strategic value of the discord between Czechs and Sudeten Germans and became publicly sympathetic to the German situation. Under the political leadership Konrad Henlein, the Sudeten Germans collectively proclaimed themselves for Germany. This event precipitated The Munich Pact, which was signed on September 30, 1938 and allowed Hitler to occupy the Sudetenland. In the agreement, France and Britain were to guarantee the new Czechoslovak borders. Thus, Mr. Henlein had practically delivered the Sudetenland to Hitler. After the war started, he was summarily demoted and spent the rest of his life in Bavaria, a forgotten man.

After The Munich Pact was signed, Czechs living in Sudetenland had to flee for their lives and so began the real fight between Czechs and Germans. When the Nazis had occupied our whole country, their rule was ruthless. One had to be constantly on guard, because some Czechs chose or were forced to cooperate with the Nazis. If you said the wrong thing in the wrong company, a Czech informant would report you to Nazi authorities. Being reported usually meant that you and your family were executed.

THE NAZIS TAKE CZECHOSLOVAKIA

By Mid-March 1939, the Nazis had completely occupied our country. Initially, I heard rumors that Hitler's army was fake and that he didn't have real tanks, guns and trucks. Some even said tanks seen at the front were made of paper. We learned the truth when the Nazi army rolled into to our diocesan city of Hradec Králové and we saw Hitler's well-organized war machine up close.

At the beginning of the invasion, the Nazis put on a deceptively kind face. They even posted signs, "This place forbidden to German soldiers" in front of beer gardens and similar establishments. However, when university students protested the occupation in Prague on November 17, 1939 the Nazis response was swift and brutal. Thousands of students were arrested and shipped to the Oranienburg concentration camp. The Nazis then abolished all Czech universities, colleges and other institutions of higher learning. That blow fell to my friend Vladislav Valach, who had been a medical student in Prague. He survived imprisonment and told me much about the camp. After the war, he went on to become a successful surgeon and authored a book on surgical procedures.

Shortly after suppressing the students in Prague, the Nazis ordered all Jews to wear the Star of David. This was just the beginning of the misery and torture of Jewish Czechoslovakians. Nazi authorities soon declared it illegal for Czechs to associate with Jews under penalty of imprisonment or worse.

Jews were forbidden to go to any public place and were allowed only one hour each day to shop. I remember feeling very sorry for one old Jewish lady. She could barely walk up the hill to buy her food at the grocery. I said "Hello" to her and tried to smile. I felt very helpless. I recall wondering how the Nazis knew who was Jewish and who was not. Their plan for the Jews had been made well in advance.

HOW THE NAZIS IDENTIFIED JEWS

The Nazis knew that Czechoslovakia had four state-supported religions. These religions were: The Evangelical Brothren, Hussite National Church, Jewish Congregations and the Catholic Church. Each of these religious organizations was a state statistical office and kept records of births, marriages and funerals. People who did not belong to one of these religions had to register at their county courthouse.

When someone wanted to quit their church, they had to write to the county courthouse. The courthouse would then notify the church that that person no longer wanted to be a member. This procedure did not work for Jews during the occupation. Very early on, the Nazi SS visited Rabbis in every town and demanded lists of all

Jews. These lists were used to identify Jews, who were then ordered to wear the Star of David.

When the Nazis had everything in order, they quietly and systematically instructed the Jews in each town to come to the nearest railroad station at 3 or 4 o'clock in the morning, carrying one bag. Almost no one but the Jews knew of these instructions. In town after town and city after city, it was as if all the Jews just disappeared, overnight. They were told that they were being moved to "Work Camps."

During most of the war, I lived and worked at the Provostship in Litomyšl. Before the invasion, Litomyšl was home to about 30 Jewish families. All of these families disappeared in one night and I know of only 3 individuals that returned after the war.

I recall one terrible incident from the summer of 1942. At the railroad station in Pardubice stood two cattle cars guarded by Nazi soldiers. For several days, Czech Jews were heard crying and pleading from inside the locked cars, "Please help us. We are Czechs. We are patriots." We felt completely helpless. Any word or deed against Nazi rule was often swiftly punished by death.

Some Jews survived by being hidden by Czechs who lived well outside of towns. I heard that the well-known Jewish tenor, Jára Pospíšil hid at a secluded Czech farm and could not so much as peep. I saw him perform after the war and in my opinion his voice was not as before. He was famous in operettas like, "Merry Widow" and "Chocolate Soldier." Jara was very good in his prime.

ASSASSINATION OF HEYDRICH AND NAZI REPRISAL

The year 1942 was critical for the Czech nation. The Nazis were winning on all sides and becoming drunk with their power. The assassination of Reichsprotektor Reinhard Heydrich in Prague changed the Nazi situation in Czechoslovakia. By assassinating one of Hitler's most valued officers, the Czech resistance demonstrated its own power.

Reinhard Heydrich was known by many nicknames, such as "Bloody Dog," "The Butcher of Prague" and "The Blond Beast." He was very close to Hitler and had been appointed Reichsprotektor of Bohemia and Moravia in September 1941. Two members of the Czech resistance managed to assassinate him in May 1942. It is a powerful and tragic story.

Many Czech patriots had fled to England in early 1941. A select group of these brave boys were taken to Canada, where a British officer trained them for special operations. Canada remained relatively free of Nazi spies and was a good location for secret training. Later that year, the Czech Special Forces traveled back to England and set about gathering intelligence from both from British sources and the Czech underground. The assassination of Heydrich was planned by Czechs and carried out with British military support. In December 1941, two Czech Special Forces officers parachuted into Nazi occupied Czechoslovakia and assassinated Heydrich in Prague.

The "Butcher of Prague" was dead. Czechs had demonstrated that the Nazis were not invincible, but reprisal was horrible. It began with a massacre in the Czech city of Lidice, where over 300 men, woman and children were shot along with a Catholic priest.

Across our country, the Nazis abducted 1000's of Czechs from their homes or on the street. Hundreds of captive Czechs endured torturous interrogation, followed by execution. In all, some 10,000 Czechs were taken to concentration camps. The Nazis declared that every house, room and hole in all of Czechoslovakia would be searched. Any Czech found without proper ID, would be shot immediately. I would learn what the Nazis meant first hand.

WITHOUT PROPER IDENTIFICATION

At the time of the Nazi crackdown, I was in my fifth class at the seminary with 12 other students. One day the classroom door burst open. Three uniformed men entered the classroom and announced that they would inspect our desks and our IDs. One of the men was a Nazi officer, another was a Nazi soldier and the third was a worried-looking Czech police officer.

The Nazi officer began questioning a seminarian named Bosina. He had a German mother and spoke the language fluently. An argument soon erupted between the two men. The Czech policeman came over to me and said, "Open your desk and show me your ID." I opened my desk and nervously told him that I did not have an ID, only my application for it. He became very concerned and we quietly discussed what to do.

As the argument between Bosina and the officer raged on, the Nazi soldier became increasingly impatient. After inspecting several of the other boy's desks, he called to the Czech policeman, "Alles in ordung?" The Czech policeman replied confidently, "Jawohl." In a flash, they were gone. The Czech police officer had risked his life to save me. I realized then, that I had risked the lives of my fellow seminarians by not having my ID. They forgave me, but I made sure my ID application got processed right away.

POPULAR SAVINGS & THE LIDICE MASSACRE

My father's bank continued business despite of the war. Around the time of my run-in with the Nazis at the seminary, my father lent some money to a Czech tool making business. With the additional capital, the toolmakers bought plates of Swedish steel, which was prized for making wood-working tools. The company quickly received orders from pump-makers, wooden-wheel-makers and even the picky violinmakers!

Shortly after Heydrich's assassination, I was at our bank when a strange letter arrived. My father's face grew grim as he read the letter. "Look what I got in the mail!" he said, showing me a list of all the men massacred in Lidice. The Nazi letter was to inform my father that if any of the dead men had bank accounts, we were to immediately send their money to Nazi authorities in Prague.

NAZI SIEGE OF A TOWN NEAR TURNOV

Nazi rule became more ruthless as time went by and Czechs were living in a constant state of fear. A friend of my father told us the following story. These events occurred in a city near Turnov, the name of which I no longer remember.

My father's friend was mushroom hunting one day when two young men confronted him. They said they'd been watching him for several hours and needed to "confirm" his name. Upon hearing his name, they handed him a letter from England. The letter was from a priest named Monsignor Sramek, who had been a Czechoslovakian political leader in 1918. He had managed to escape the country along with President Benes and was now serving as Prime Minister of our exiled government in England.

The letter read, "Dear brother, I ask that you please help these two Czech patriots." It was signed "Msgr. Josef Sramek." He studied the letter carefully. Raising his eyes back toward the men, he was confonted with two gun barrels. One of the men said, "Are you going to help us? If not, we will have to kill you, because we could be betrayed." Having little choice, he agreed to supply them with food and help them find a secure location for their operations. He told the men of a deserted swimming pool with a cabana, which lie at the farthest edge of town. In this cabana, the Czechs set-up a communications radio and began their intelligence work.

The Nazis had an excellent system for detecting clandestine radio transmissions and it didn't take them long to locate this one. They responded by surrounding the entire town with soldiers and tanks. The Mayor was instructed to go to the cabana and force the Czech "spies" to surrender. The Nazis wanted these men alive, along with their equipment and communications codes. The Mayor was informed that if the men did not surrender, the town would be leveled and all of its people killed, just like in Lidice.

Obediently, the Mayor went and asked the patriots to surrender in order to spare the town and its people. The men refused. The Mayor begged them to surrender. They explained that they could not surrender, because it was forbidden to place the encryption codes at risk. The Mayor finally went down on his knees and pleaded with the men, "Please, for the sake of our woman and children, and the innocent people of this town, you must give yourselves up!"

Unable to bear this burden, the two patriots reluctantly agreed to surrender. They destroyed their equipment and the encryption codes. Then to the Mayor's horror, each man took a pill from his pocket, bit into it and died. The Nazi commander was very angry that the men were not taken alive, but the town was spared.

NAZI OCCUPATION & MY ARRIVAL IN LITOMYŠL

The Nazi occupation eventually had a direct affect on me. Because Catholic priests were government employees, before ordination to the priesthood I had to complete papers assuring my Aryan ancestry. In accordance with Hitler's decree, non-Aryan people were not eligible to hold government positions. I was hoping a Czech clerk would let the matter go, but that didn't happen.

One of my grandmothers was German, but the other had been Jewish. Some Nazi clerk had underlined that fact twice in red pencil on my ancestry form, summarily rejecting my application. I would not be paid as a priest. The Bishop offered to ordain me and have me remain in his care (od mensam episcopi), but that did not appeal to me. I was now a deacon. I could baptize, marry and bury people, so I decided to continue my unpaid duties and wait. Eventually, I was offered positions in Breslaum, Germany and Litomyšl, Czechoslovakia.

I selected Litomyšl, where Th.D. Pastor Josef Durek was anxious to have me improve his church music programs. I came to Litomyšl in November 1942 and stayed for 7 years. Just 24 years old, I could not have imagined the important role Pastor Durek would play in my life. Sadly, our relationship would end in some tragedy. My time in Litomyšl was the most dangerous and edifying period of my life.

When the Austro-Hungarian Empire collapsed in 1918, Pope Benedict XV requested an audience with Pastor Durek. The Pope knew that Pastor Durek would give him an accurate assessment of the state of the Catholic Church in the changing political environment. The Pope was so pleased with Pastor Durek's work that he granted him 300,000 lira to build a Catholic youth hall in Litomyšl. This hall stands today as a monument to my mentor and friend, Josef Durek.

In Litomyšl, as throughout occupied Europe, the Nazis stole whatever they needed for the war effort. They collected metal and cloth, tires from cars and even confiscated the bells from churches all over the country. Such actions infuriated Czechs. Fearing revolution, the Nazis forbade Czech from gathering in groups.

As a result, in 1944 they forbade the procession for the feast of Corpus Christi. We were determined to have it in Litomyšl. With the permission and blessing of Pastor Durek, I went to the county offices and talked to the highest Czech officer. He was willing to chance a special request for us.

Together we filed an application with the Gestapo and the Kreis Rat in Pardubice. We respectfully explained to the Nazis that our country was very Catholic and allowing the Corpus Christi procession would be greatly appreciated by the people of Litomyšl. To our amazement, permission was granted for the "Frohleichnam Procession." I was personally responsible for organizing the event and keeping it peaceful. I selected uplifting music for the city band to play. For one golden day in 1944, everything was as it was before.

Me at the Litomyšl Provostship age 28.

My first Mass procession celebration in Litomysl.

Giving my first Mass. Pastor Durek is to my right.

NAZIS FORCE CZECHS INTO LABOR

By 1944, the Nazis were getting short on labor. They ordered all Czech boys and girls born in 1920 into forced labor in Germany or digging ditches on various fronts. In order to protect German citizens, Czech youths were forced to work in factories and other places directly in the path of Allied bombers. By the end of the war, the Nazis had taken thousands of Czech youths to far-reaching parts of Europe.

Eventually, my birth year (1918) was called to forced labor. Twice, I reported to the Nazi draft board in the town of Litomyšl only to be deferred because I was a priest. I felt bad when others had to go and I was deferred. I learned later that some Germans and Czechs from Litomyšl quietly saw to it that I was not taken. Feeling guilty, I decided to register in the town of Turnov where almost no one knew me. My draft call soon came. As fate would have it, I was to have another fortunate encounter with the Nazis.

MY FORCED LABOR DRAFT

I waited in front of the hall and asked the other guys about the situation inside. I was told that the doctor who would examine me was a Sudeten German. In the hall were nine tables, each manned by an older German soldier. If the doctor sent you to the first three tables, then you were forced into labor. If you were sent to the next three tables, you might be deferred. If the doctor sent you to the last 3 tables, you were free! Suddenly, my guilty feelings about deferment were completely gone.

I stood in front of the doctor and said to him in German, "Doctor, you must help me. I am a Catholic priest." I took the chance, because I was a deacon. The doctor looked shocked and I watched him become more anxious by the moment. He took some extra time to examine me and finally wrote, "Priest" on my papers, ironically underlining the word twice with a red pencil. He sent me to the last three tables.

"So, you do not want to go?" asked the old German soldier at table No. 8. I responded in German, "Oh yes! I want to go, but I cannot." "Why?" he insisted. "Because, I am doing a very important job for the German Reich." I declared. All three soldiers looked at each other, puzzled. "What kind of a job?" He asked dismissively. "I am doing the statistics." I answered with perfect confidence. I hung all my hopes on this one word, a word that seemed very important to every German. The soldier looked dazed. Sensing that my bluff was working, I continued. "I am at a parish of 10,000 souls. I am in charge of the office and responsible for all of the statistics, like births, marriages and deaths, even for the brave German soldiers. My reports are sent to the German statistical office in Prague each month." The soldier smiled at his colleagues again then shouted, "Gehen Sie!" (Get Lost!) I did!

Most Czech priests were not so lucky and found themselves in Berlin repairing roofs after Allied bombing raids. It was very hard work and they were constantly hungry, but being Czechs they had a solution. When they smelled food being cooked by the Housefraus in the kitchen below, they blocked the chimney with wood. Her kitchen would soon begin to fill with smoke and she would run outdoors to ask the priests to investigate the problem. After some commotion, the wood was removed from the chimney. Such wily priests were often rewarded with fresh kuchen cake!

I would like to conclude this chapter with a story that is short, but very important to me. Shortly after I came to America, I met an American soldier who had faced the Nazis across the river Rhine. I asked him, "Did you shoot at the Germans?" "No," he answered, "They also wanted to live."

HITLER'S PLAN FOR CZECHS

It is a sad fact that during the war, Czechs were not allowed University study. I believe this was an indication of Hitler's intention to rearrange the people of Europe after he won the war. Czechs commonly believed that Hitler planned to resettle the whole nation, some 10 million souls, to Siberia. Today, we know that he could have accomplished this using cattle cars as he did with the Jews. Most Catholic priests believed that Hitler intended to erase the Catholic Church and all priests from Europe. Thank God it never came to that.

CZECH RESISTANCE TRAINED IN ENGLAND

The conditions in our country were truly terrible. Hitler now called Czechoslovakia "The Protectorate of Bohemia and Moravia," after granting "freedom" to Sudetenland and Slovakia and erasing Carpatho-Ruthenia forever. Our people responded in the only way they could, by organizing an underground resistance. Unfortunately, the resistance was fractured into two parts. The Czech patriots that had fled to England and Canada led one underground resistance movement. Russian partisans led the other underground movement. Each movement had different goals, which significantly complicated our national situation.

Like those who assassinated Heydrich, Czechs in England and Canada underwent special training in preparation to return as a powerful resistance force. They intended to parachute back into Czechoslovakia and rally the nation to fight the Nazis. Tragically, these brave boys were betrayed long before they jumped back inside the Nazi lines.

Following the assassination of Heydrich, the Nazis fortified their spy rings in England and were able to monitor the staging activities of Czech resistance forces. The hard work of those brave Czechs was practically for naught. When they did parachute back into the country, the Nazis were expecting them. Those who were not captured and killed were in constant hiding from the Gestapo.

CZECH RESISTANCE BY RUSSIAN PARTISANS

The situation was completely different with the Russian partisans. Groups of Russian partisans traveled by foot and lived in the forest. They moved often and kept a very low profile, but constantly collected intelligence information. A group of about 15 lived near Litomyšl. One day, the wife of a school principal from a nearby village came to our parish house. She carried a message from the Russians. They needed food and blankets and would pay handsomely for weapons.

She told us that the Russians had two leaders. Sasha was the group commander. The other leader was a commissar, whose duty it was to gather information about the area for future political and military maneuvers. Sasha wanted me to make contact with another group of Russian partisans, led by a Major. We knew of him from another source; a man who operated the railroad telegraph in Chocen, near Horní Jelení.

The railroad telegraph became a very important means of underground communication during the Nazi occupation. Railroad telegraph lines were separate from public lines and not easily monitored by Nazi authorities. The Nazis resisted tampering with the railroad system, because commerce depended on reliable communications. Therefore, it became an excellent way for the resistance to communicate in secrecy.

I spoke to the telegraph man and he was willing to arrange a meeting between the Russian Major and myself. He said to me, "You must know that if you do not work with him, he is obliged to shoot you on the spot, because if you were caught and talked he would be betrayed." The choice was clear. I couldn't risk my life for the Russians.

31

MY VOW OF NON-VIOLENCE

The question of when it is necessary to kill is the greatest moral dilemma, especially for a priest. Wartime cast me into many situations involving decisions of life and death. I vowed never to participate in anything that could result in a death, no matter how beneficial it may be to a cause. This vow has served my heart, my profession and my soul well. Not all priests were so fortunate. I remember one very public example in Bavaria, where Cardinal Doepfner suffered great indignation after appointing a priest and consecrating him as a Bishop in Munich.

I have forgotten this priest's name, but during the war he was a German officer stationed in Italy. He commanded a section where the Italian underground was very active. During his command, eleven members of the Italian underground were captured and condemned to death. As commander, he received orders to execute the Italians. Twice he refused his orders. When the third order came, he chose to resign his command rather than be responsible for the execution.

His resignation meant little and the Italians were executed anyway. After the war, he attended the seminary and became a priest. When the Italian people learned that Cardinal Doepfner had consecrated him as a Bishop, it caused a national furor. Many Italians protested the Vatican directly. As a result, the new Bishop was never permitted to work in his commission.

These events affected Cardinal Doepfner deeply and I believe he died of a broken heart. I knew the Cardinal well and corresponded with him for many years. When I first met him, I was a Czech refugee and he was the Bishop of Wurzburg. If not for his kindness and support, my life would have been very different. He helped me greatly in my time of need and I came to be fond of him. He went on to become the Bishop of Berlin, which at that time was an extremely difficult assignment. The present Holy Father, Pope Benedict XVI, followed Cardinal Doepfner in Munich.

THE PROVOSTSHIP

The final months of the war were full of danger and adventure. Our parish house was large enough for six people: three priests, a housekeeper, maid, and a janitor. Two other rooms were loaned to the Inspector of Schools. Pastor Durek supported cancer research, so two rooms were loaned to a pair of medical doctors who were researching the use of viper venom to cure cancer. One day a large crate arrived for the doctors. When they opened it there was yelling and great commotion. The crate contained live vipers! The doctors had expected dead snakes.

Our last little room was occupied by a man in hiding from the Nazis. He was affiliated with the Allies and had financial support from England. We all knew him, but never spoke of it. He had harbored several English parachutists on his farm, but the Nazis had discovered them. He escaped, but his wife and her father were captured and taken to a concentration camp. Only she survived.

A high-ranking underground leader had asked Pastor Durek to give this man refuge. I carried food to him 3 times a day and cut his hair when he needed. Eventually, the Nazis began to search Litomyšl and promised to kill everyone without proper ID. We knew we had to get him out of the Provostship. After some searching and quiet negotiation, we found a farmer in the country who was willing to take him. The main problem was how to get him out of town, as the SS constantly patrolled our streets. We devised "The Bicycle Plan."

I went first on my bicycle, wearing my collar and riding casually. After I had covered a short distance, the harbored man followed on another bicycle. Our janitor brought up the rear, so he could report back if disaster occurred. Naturally, we encountered a SS patrol of 6 men. Thankfully, they let us all pass without incident. We were very lucky.

Several days later, a cherished member of our congregation was stopped while riding his bicycle into town. The SS searched him and found a Czechoslovak flag in his bag. For carrying this flag he was taken directly to the Nazi post and publicly hanged. This man had a wife and 5 children. Such brutality is completely unimaginable.

The final days of the war were very dangerous. Czechoslovakia became a last refuge for Hitler's army, which was now losing on all sides. Prague alone was occupied by over 200,000 Nazi troops. The Czech people were very anxious to see the Germans go. No one knew that another occupier was coming.

CHAPTER 3

THE CIRCLE CLOSES

THE PRAGUE UPRISING

The Czech national situation became increasingly complicated and frustrating as the war came to a close. We didn't realize that the Allies and Stalin would yet transform the map of Europe. The Czech nation was anticipating liberation, but it was not to be. The American army had advanced to within 25 kilometers west of Prague, but was not allowed to enter the city and help. The Soviet Red army had advanced to within 20 kilometers east of Prague, but did not want help. Stalin hoped that Czech resistance against the Germans in Prague would fail, as the Polish resistance in Warsaw had failed.

A key member of the Czech revolution committee was a close friend of mine. He organized what has become known as the "Prague Uprising." He once told me that he received intelligence from England that was invaluable in planning the uprising. On May 5, 1945, he gave the order, "The action against German forces will begin now." The message was carried by Czech national radio.

Our tired nation held its collective breath as eight Czech policemen began a strategic revolt against the Nazis in Prague. First, the policemen tried to capture a powerful radio station in Prague, from which they could broadcast further instructions and stir the nation to revolt. Using a heavy truck, they crashed through the gate of the radio station building. Intelligence estimates indicated that about 30 SS troops would be guarding the station. The policemen encountered over 70 SS troops. So began the Prague Uprising.

One Czech radio station employee stayed on the air, while other employees tried to assist the policemen. The situation soon became dire. The SS called for reinforcements and Nazi soldiers soon arrived with tanks. Responding to word of the revolt, thousands of Czech citizens flooded into the streets of Prague. They surrounded

Nazi positions and made thousands of barricades from furniture, cars and streetcars. Two things helped the uprising. First, Czech utility system workers began to cut-off the Nazi's water, electricity and telephone communications. Second, a group of Czech boys reported to Czech authorities that while exploring a nearby barracks they had found German "rockets." With men standing guard, the boys crawled back into the barracks and returned with boxes of what were actually German anti-tank weapons. Czech resistance fighters used these weapons to disable many German tanks.

By May 7, 1945, about 1,500 citizens of Prague had died in the uprising. Most fought with nothing but their bare hands. Fearing that the Czechs might prevail, Nazi tank divisions outside Prague moved forward and began shelling. Soon, the Luftwaffe began dropping bombs on our beautiful city. It became evident that the Nazis were still too powerful to beat. Just when the uprising seemed doomed to fail, a miracle occurred!

Hiding 10 miles east of Prague was Vlasov's Army. Unknown to all but a few Czechs, Vlasov's Army was the Russian anti-communist liberation army, lead by General Andrey Vlasov. It seems the Czech revolution committee had a friend in Vlasov's Army. First division commander General Sergei Bunyachenko was granted permission to lead his men into Prague to help the Czechs. About 20,000 of General Bunyachenko's well-equipped men entered Prague and flatly defeated the Nazis.

My friend in the revolution committee told me what happened next. A Nazi commander contacted the committee and offered a deal that would save Prague from further destruction. If the Nazis were given an escape corridor to the north, they would evacuate peacefully. An agreement was made and the German army, along with some 100,000 German civilians marched out of Prague.

Thanks to Generals Vlasov and Bunyachenko, the Prague Uprising had succeeded, but all was not as it seemed. The Czech revolt had expelled the Germans and saved the great city from ruin. However, we were not to liberate ourselves from Communist Russia.

Vlasov's Army left Prague just before Stalin's Red Army "liberated" Czechoslovakia on May 9, 1945. I was in Prague that day and saw many limousines enter the presidential palace. Those cars carried Soviet generals who were invited by Czech leaders to a banquet celebrating the liberation of Czechoslovakia. I did not recognize the irony of the situation at the time.

On May 10, 1945, Vlasov's army surrendered to Allied forces in hopes of gaining asylum, which would protect them from Stalin. During the course of delicate negotiations with the Allies, General Vlasov was captured by Soviet troops. In a matter of days, the Soviets had executed or imprisoned almost 200,000 of Vlasov's men. General Vlasov was hanged on August 1, 1946. Our nation remembers the brave soldiers of Vlasov's Army very fondly.

TENSIONS IN LITOMYŠL

Litomyšl, being the first major Czech city east of Sudetenland, was full of German soldiers and other refugees. The Germans had a Catholic military chaplain from Munich, named Josef Thanbichler. He had taught at the seminary in Munich, but was now living with the German soldiers in an abandoned school. He visited the Provostship frequently and we became friends.

The Germans also had a military lazaret and when any German soldier died, Father Thanbichler brought his name to us to be recorded. Many dead German soldiers were buried in our cemetery. Dead Russian POWs were not so lucky. Hundreds of Russian soldiers were buried without ceremony at the wall of the cemetery.

It seemed like a million Russian POWs were marched through Litomyšl. Many of the men were little more than walking skeletons, terribly hungry and sick. At first Czechs threw bread into their lines, but this caused the hungry men to fight. The Germans allowed us to feed their hungry men, but only in an organized and supervised fashion. We were otherwise forbidden to approach the Germans.

On one occasion, Russian POWs were marching past the house where a Nazi commander and his wife were living. His wife threw bread to the starving men and as usual they fought over it. The commander became very angry. He rushed outside and began to beat the men with the butt of his rifle. The gun accidentally fired, hitting the commander in the head and killing him instantly.

The underground Russian partisans knew of my contact with Father Thanbichler and asked me to give him this message, "Go to the Nazi Commander and tell him that if all Germans soldiers drop their weapons, the Russians will allow them safe exit." I obediently gave Father Thanbichler the message, but he refused to relay it to the Nazi high Command. I was somewhat relieved, because if the Germans had complied the Russian partisans would have had many weapons, placing both Czechs and Germans in even greater danger.

A short time later, Father Thanbichler came to say goodbye to me. He told me that the whole German army planned to go to Bavaria, where it could surrender to American forces. Naturally, the position of the Russian partisans quickly changed. They suddenly demanded all Nazi soldiers to remain in Litomyšl, claiming that the Germans now had to act in accordance with Russian interests. Thus I watched power shift from Nazi control to Russian Communist control. Months later, I received a postcard from Moscow. Father Thanbichler had become a POW. After I escaped in 1949, I found him Munich.

THE COMMUNIST REVOLUTION

Litomyšl was the only county in Bohemia where the Communists lost in the "free" elections of 1946. However, we did not have a strong personality to install as Chairman of the county. Pastor Durek was very frustrated by this problem. He was the party rainmaker and had to accept a Chairman not at all to his liking. His concern was muted in February 1948 when the Communists staged a putch and formally took power in Czechoslovakia. They immediately abolished all existing political parties and allowed only 3 new "Action" parties: The Social Democratic Party, The Socialist Party and The New Popular Party. At the time, I didn't know what was so "New" about our Popular Party. I would learn soon enough.

THE CZECH UNDERGROUND

Because the Popular Party was so strong in Litomyšl, we continued Catholic Action, especially for youths. In March 1948, we held a large Catholic Action meeting in our Parish Hall. As usual, I organized the event. I also entertained on piano and lead the singing. Pastor Durek invited Josef Hosticka to be our main speaker. Mr. Hosticka was an attorney and a founding member of the New Popular Party in Prague. To our delight and surprise, over 800 young people attended the event.

The day began with Mass, followed by a large luncheon. In the afternoon, we had some excellent musical entertainment and youth activities. Josef Hosticka closed the event with a speech emphasizing the importance of Catholic faith and the New Popular Party. Most attendees agreed that Mr. Hosticka's speech was excellent. It was not overtly anti-Communist, but it gave us hope for the future.

Mr. Hosticka was most impressed with the turnout. He took me aside and said, "You have a real powerhouse here. We'll need the support of these young people in the future." He also told me what was "New" about the Popular Party. Against all odds, he and others had successfully negotiated for the party's continued existence with the secret purpose of working against the Communists as an underground movement. Mr. Hosticka was secretly a powerful member of the Czech underground and on this March afternoon, he invited me to join the movement.

Naturally, Pastor Durek encouraged me to do what he could not. He knew he was too high profile and perhaps a little too old to work in the underground. With Pastor Durek's blessing, I accepted

39

Mr. Hosticka's invitation. Days later, a professor from a local school visited Pastor Durek and recommended one of his former students as my collaborator. Her name was Marie Sedlackova. Interestingly, Litomyšl had two important underground members by that name.

One Marie Sedlackova had been active during the war and was involved in the assassination of Reinhardt Heydrich. For this, the Gestapo executed her. The other Marie Sedlackova, who became my collaborator, was a very important agent in our underground movement. On one occasion, she gave me almost one million Czech crowns belonging to her uncle.

The Communists had confiscated most of her uncle's money, but he had maintained this secret cache of crowns. The problem was that the Czech crown was no longer legal currency. Any attempt to use crowns for commerce was punishable by imprisonment. Churches were one of the few organizations allowed to exchange crowns for the new Communist currency. Thanks to Marie Sedlackova, I had plenty of money to travel and provide support to Czech families with fathers in Communist prisons.

UNDERGROUND OPERATIONS

My vow of non-violence was tested soon after the Communist revolution of 1948. Immediately following the revolution, many people began to escape from Czechoslovakia. Among the first people to escape were politically experienced Czechs who realized the treacherous implications of Communist rule.

A group of politically savvy Czech refugees established a secret committee that met at the Goetheschule in Regensburg, Germany. I know the names of only two committee members, Mr. Randolf and Father Petr Lekavy. The Regensburg committee supported Czech interests and coordinated special operations against the Communist regime through the Czech underground. One such operation involved another Czech refugee. Known to me only as "Choc," he had been a university student in Prague before escaping to Germany.

I saw Choc only once, but never met him personally. If I had met him, you would not be reading this book.

When the Communists took power, some Czech officials tried to hold onto their government positions. Foreign Minister Jan Masaryk, son of former President Tomáš Masaryk, was one of those people. Jan Masaryk died mysteriously in March 1948. Many in the Czech underground suspected that a Russian Major named Schram had murdered him. To this day, no one can confirm the cause of Jan Masaryk's death. In the fog of revolution, underground reprisal for the suspected murder was obligatory.

The Regensburg committee found Choc to be an eager assassin. They arranged for his return to Prague and gave him a message to take to the head of the Czech underground. Choc carried this message in the heel of his shoe. The message contained an order and key instructions for the assassination of Major Schram. Several committee members signed the order in code.

Once back in Prague, Choc quietly made contact with the Czech underground. He received word that the head of the underground would meet him in Prague. Choc may have known that his contact was also the General Secretary of the New Popular Party. What he didn't know was the General Secretary was meeting him personally, because I had refused to.

Days earlier, the General Secretary had summoned me to Prague for a top-secret meeting. During this meeting, I learned that Choc might be part of an assassination plot. The General Secretary said, "We need you to meet with Choc and collect a message that he carries." Honoring my vow, I refused to attend the meeting. I would not be part of a killing. The General Secretary did convince me to accompany him to the meeting place and I stood watch across the street. They met near the National Museum in Prague. I saw Choc give his message to the General Secretary. He never knew I was there.

With approval from the General Secretary and intelligence from the Czech underground, Choc found Major Schram and killed him. He escaped the scene, but was caught some days later in Moravia where he was tortured and executed. While being tortured, Choc had given the Communist police much information. Some 80 people who knew Choc were given harsh prison sentences. The General Secretary underwent ruthless Soviet interrogation, but he never betrayed me. He was sentenced to 27 years in prison. Again, I was spared.

FAILED UPRISINGS

The backlash from Major Schram's assassination somewhat crippled our underground movement. The fate of special committee member Randolf is unknown to me. Father Lekavy was more fortunate. He became Pontifical Delegate for Catholic priests in the German refugee camps. I was to have an auspicious meeting with him a few years later, as he fulfilled his duties in a German camp.

Indeed, the Communist regime proved to be very strong. I knew of plans for two underground uprisings, but both failed. The first plan involved a Czech who had become the commander of a tank division. He was willing to start an uprising. However, during the planning phase of this operation his wife became suspicious of his frequent meetings and hired a private detective to follow him. The private detective was a Communist informant who immediately reported him, foiling the uprising.

The second uprising was tentatively scheduled for December 24, 1948. I had little specific knowledge of this plan, but was told to expect a coded telegram with instructions. The telegram never came and the uprising never occurred. It remains a mystery to this day, but I feel strongly that someone betrayed the second plan. Informants were everywhere. Years later, I asked an American CIC agent about it, but knew even less than I.

On one occasion in 1948, I visited the American Embassy in Prague on behalf of the Czech underground. A British lawyer named Pinkas who was fluent in both Czech and English accompanied me. Apparently, I made a good impression on the Americans.

My name was given to an American named Mr. Sullivan, who was then director of Catholic relief services in Prague. He was later proclaimed "persona non grata" by the Communists and forced to flee to Frankfort, Germany. After escaping, Mr. Sullivan sent word to my friends in Prague, "Tell Father Marek that if he can make it to Germany, I will look after him."

THE SURFACING UNDERGROUND

Even with the failed uprisings, the Czech underground continued to grow and along with it the danger of being infiltrated by Communist secret police. The Communists had much more experience with underground movements than we. History has shown that they were masters of working against governments all over the world.

In late 1948, I met with an underground group based in east Bohemia. They had tapped into communications between the Communist secret police via a teletype operator in Pardubice. We soon learned what the police intended to do with Catholic priests who did not cooperate. It was a sobering and vile gambit.

A letter of deception and slander was sent from Prague to all the county chairmen of the Communist Party. By this letter, it became official Communist policy to discredit Catholic priests by all possible means. The chairmen were to spread propaganda about the weakness and hypocrisy of Catholic priests. We were accused of excessive drinking, womanizing, hording collection money and using our positions for purely political motives.

Fortunately, this policy had little impact on the church faithful. I knew of only three priests in our diocese that felt threatened enough to cooperate with the Communists. Such aggressive strategies often backfired on the Communists. Even those they imprisoned sometimes found ways to help the underground. One such prisoner tried to save me from abduction.

ESCAPE WARNING

It was around midnight, sometime in December 1948, when a man from the east Bohemia underground rang the bell at our Provostship. I went down and opened the gate. He looked very worried and said, "Father, please help me. I must escape to Germany immediately." He told me how two weeks earlier, two young men had paid him a surprise visit. They had identified themselves as members of our underground and even used the most current codes. Even so, he'd felt suspicion and told them to return in two weeks time.

When they returned, a beautiful young woman accompanied them. They wanted to contact a particular member of the Slovakian underground, a person whom he had specific knowledge. After making their request the men returned to their car, leaving the young woman alone in his company. If this was intentional or not, one can only speculate today. He explained to the woman that he was a married man with two daughters about her age.

Upon hearing this, the woman said there was something she wanted to tell him, but he must first swear on his life not to betray her. He promised. She said, "Those two men are from the Communist secret police and I am their prisoner. They use me to make men talk and I cooperate because it is the only way I can warn people like you." His suspicions had been valid. She continued, "You must escape immediately to Germany. Please quietly inform Father Marek that he too is in great danger and must escape as soon as possible." These words cast a shadow of darkness over my heart. For many years, I tried to learn the identity of that brave woman. Her name and her story shall always be a mystery to me.

Conditions in Communist prisons were particularly cruel and the guards were known for their utter brutality. Communist prison guards routinely forced old and sickly priests to stand outside in the cold and completely disrobe. Sometimes they were forced to stand at attention for hours or until they fell. People have asked me, "Who was worse, the Nazis or the Communists?" Such inhumanity has no Earthly measure.

44

CHAPTER 4

ABDUCTION & ESCAPE

ABDUCTED BY THE COMMUNISTS

Heeding the woman's warning, I began to investigate escape options, but it was too late. On the first day of February 1949, the Communist police came looking for me. The story begins in the tiny village of Trstenice, where I taught a religion class at the public school. We called the practice of teaching in neighboring parishes "Excurrendo" meaning, "running from the town to the country."

The school in Trstenice was divided almost equally between Communist and Catholic youths. The older Communist pupils had become very politically active, demonstrating the powerful influence of Communist propaganda and Pioneer Groups on Czech youth. As I was leaving the classroom one day, a boy shouted, "They say that Christ was the first Communist!" On another occasion, a great fight erupted between the Communist boys and Catholic boys. I was pleased to hear that the Catholics had prevailed. Naturally, I said not a word.

It was about 4 o'clock in the afternoon when after finishing the Trstenice class, I stopped at our nearby parish house to see my parents who happened to be visiting. Bidding my father farewell and kissing my mother's cheek, I made my way toward the bus station. A car suddenly appeared. I could see that it contained five uniformed men. I immediately realized that my time had come.

The doors of the car flew open as it screeched to a halt beside me. Two men jumped out. One man was a uniformed Communist policeman. The other was the County Chairman of the Communist Party. The Chairman demanded, "What is your name?" "Father Walter Marek," I answered politely. School children were walking past and I saw bewilderment in their eyes, as they wondered what was happening to me. The Chairman said, "You will get in the car and go with them." With this, he and the other officer turned toward the bus station. I was pulled into the back seat of the car and the door was slammed shut.

A secret policeman sat next to me. Another secret policeman and the driver occupied the front seat. The driver was a young man who had been in my Catholic youth group. I heard that he had married a Catholic girl and become a loyal Communist. These facts encouraged me to talk to him. I asked him how he was. He was so embarrassed by the circumstances that he could not speak. Undeterred, I asked each policeman where he came from. It was important to know if they had come from Prague or from the regional office in Pardubice.

As our car passed the bus station, I could see that the Chairman and officer had stopped another car. It was our car from the Provostship. Our janitor was behind the wheel and Pastor Durek was in the back seat. Apparently, the police had stopped first in Litomyšl looking for me. Learning of this, Pastor Durek had rushed to Trstenice to warn me. The men commandeered their car and turned toward Litomyšl. We followed close behind. Many thoughts went through my mind during the 40-minute ride back to Litomyšl. I quietly prayed for strength and serenity. I could only wait.

We arrived in Litomyšl at about 5:30 p.m. They took me to my room and said that I had to be questioned and my belongings searched. I felt no intimidation. I could see that they were not real detectives, but newly made Communist policemen with little experience. However, they seemed to have been trained in Catholic terminology, as they used words like "breviary" and expressions unknown to most Catholics of the day. Their questions were prepared and I anticipated many of them. My answers were mostly, "No" and excusive. They seemed particularly interested in my written sermons and preparations for catechism.

Finally, they found some English money in one of my books and asked how I'd gotten it. In the end, they had two main questions. First, was I a member of Catholic Action? Second, was I a member of Blue Angle? I answered yes to the first question and no to the second. I claimed no knowledge of Blue Angle. In fact, I'd heard that Blue Angle was a powerful anti-Communist organization reaching from Spain to Moscow. Rumor had it that the Jesuits in New York City controlled Blue Angle.

It was very cold in my room and the men were obviously tired and hungry. When they uncovered a bottle of liquor, I offered them each a drink. One policeman, who by chance would soon follow me downstairs, took two large swallows. Naturally, I took none.

The questioning concluded after about an hour when the officer said to me, "I cannot understand how a priest can lie?" One of the other men had told me that this man's wife was Catholic and he was Slovak. I taunted him saying, "Your wife would not be too proud of you calling a Catholic priest a liar!" The third man's eyes were completely vacant. He seemed well beyond disinterest and barely awake.

Finally, the officer told me it was time to leave. He said that I would not be sleeping at home that night, so I should collect some items to take with me. This helped me greatly. I pretended to search for my winter stockings in one place after another, which gave me precious time to think. I casually told the officer that I would have to gather some other items from downstairs. The man who had enjoyed two swallows of my liquor, followed me downstairs and dropped lazily onto a kitchen chair.

ESCAPE FROM LITOMYŠL

I knew that I had to escape immediately. As I walked past the rectory offices, I heard Pastor Durek shouting at the County Chairman. When I opened the back door, the cold air seemed to pull the air right out of my lungs. It was winter and in my haste I'd forgotten my coat. I realized that it hung in the kitchen, right above the policeman's head. I stopped and looked at him for a moment. He was half asleep from drink and paying no attention. My coat contained my ID, but I could not risk rousing him.

I turned and went into the utility room. There hung the winter coat of our janitor with a scarf and hat. I quickly donned his cloths and slipped silently out the back door, crouching toward the backyard gate. The watchdog saw me and thankfully did not make a sound. My hands ached with cold as I struggled to force open the frozen iron gate. It finally broke free and I fell forward onto the street. Several people greeted me and stopped to chat, having no idea what was going on. I excused myself and hurried away. The life I had known was no more.

Somehow, my mind floated far above my body. Feelings of fear, excitement, uncertainty and sadness filled me. Much of my heart was in the Litomyšl Provostship. I wanted to preserve our theatre, orchestra, and youth choirs. I enjoyed my important work in the underground. I suddenly missed Pastor Durek and all my friends in town. I wondered what would happen to them now. Pressed against the frigid February wind, a harsh and sobering memory suddenly came to me.

Pastor Durek at center and I on his right. Right rear: Janitor with no coat. Dog that didn't bark!

I had an informer in the Communist Party. This man had once come to me for advice. He wanted to open a small shop in Litomyšl, but only Communist party members were allowed to do such things. He did not want to join, but felt that he must for the good of his family. I told him to join the party and attend all of the meetings faithfully. This he did, but as time passed he said to me quite often, "Father, the Communists will destroy you." I would not see Litomyšl again for more than 40 years.

ESCAPE TO GERMAN IN 1949

My escape into Germany took over 6 weeks, during which time I faced many dangers. I finally arrived at the home of Mr. Spacek, who at great personal risk harbored me from the Communists. The relatively comfortable life I had known at the Provostship was long gone. I was now in hiding and had to wait patiently for the Czech underground to find me safe passage across the German border. With all the horror Hitler had wrought upon the world, I could never have imagined that my life would soon be in the hands of a former Nazi.

The winter of 1949 was very hard in Europe. My underground connections had chosen a German to assist me, but he could not come until the weather improved. I learned that he was a former Luftwaffe pilot who was now making a good living smuggling Czech cigarettes and people like me across the border. I was told that he was very well versed in border crossing. I could only hope this was true.

In late February, he received a telegram in Germany. The telegram informed him that his aunt was very sick and that he should come quickly. He replied by telegram that regretfully, he would not be able to come. In fact, this was the coded message to come and get me. About a week later we received information on the rendezvous. Mr. Spacek was very brave and offered to take me to the location on his motorcycle. After fortifying himself with beer he said, "If we are stopped by the police, I will talk and you will not." With these words, we roared off into the falling night.

We arrived at the rendezvous point at 8 o'clock and it was already pitch dark. All I know is that we were somewhere near the East German border, under a large tree. My German savior was clearly suspicious of me and I of him. He immediately demanded my 10,000 Czech crowns and I handed the money over. His order to me was, "Step lightly and never utter a word." Stowing the cache of crowns in his bag, he smiled and said, "At night the sound carries and also the foot steps."

Two other men joined us. I had met one of the men before. The other man came with his bicycle. Many worries filled my mind. I wondered if any of these men could be trusted. I wondered if the Communists knew about this escape path and were monitoring it. I knew the Communists operated many false American stations on the German border, where they routinely caught people trying to escape. By any measure, escaping was very dangerous. I simply had to have faith.

In an ironic turn of circumstances, Germans became very trustworthy after the war. Many Czech Communists offered phony escape services. They would meet would-be escapees, take their money and walk them right into the hands of the Communist police. Very often, desperate people who had paid all of their money to escape were betrayed by Czech informants and taken to prison in Prague. This fate had befallen a man I knew in Pardubice. He came one day to the Provostship smiling and buoyant, and said goodbye to all of us. Weeks later we received word that he was in a Communist prison. I once saw an excellent film about his story, but I no longer recall the title.

We had many, many miles to cover. Whenever we were moved for safety's sake, we stopped at a crowded tavern. It was in these taverns that our German guide would make connections and plans for our next move. He always insisted that I not speak, because I might betray myself. Sometimes this was very difficult. People in beer joints often start talking about religion and God, and not always in a respectful manner. I could not help that I was a priest. In these situations, my guide always looked at me very sternly, reminding me to remain silent. This simple fact, that I could be betrayed by my religious beliefs or my ascent, was dehumanizing. Once in America, people found my accent interesting and asked me about it. Thankfully, in America I was free to speak and worship.

We walked a tortuous route eastward and for many hours saw little but forest. Finally, we came upon a sign written in German. As we neared the border, a German policeman shadowed us for about 3 miles. The policeman made it clear that if the Communist border guards saw us, they would charge across the border and force us back into Czechoslovakia at gunpoint.

After what seemed like an eternity, we came upon a quaint German village where we registered as refugees. I felt such relief that my legs almost buckled beneath me. At last, I was free from the Communists. In a small building on the far edge of the village, we each gave our name, time of crossing and other basic information to an older German woman. The other men both carried IDs. Unfortunately, mine was still in Litomyšl.

REFUGEE WITHOUT ID

Once registered as refugees from Czechoslovakia, the German Republic provided us with protection and support. The Mayor of the village gave us directions to the closest refugee processing center, where we would be provided with shelter and food. I was very excited to be free from the Communists, but those first days in Germany were very hard indeed.

A small group of us made our way to the refugee center on foot. It was very cold and we were all without food or money. For a while we tried hitchhiking, but no one would stop for us. After walking all day, we finally found the refugee center. We were dead tired, shivering and hungry, but free. I stayed there for only one night. The following morning, I was given a railroad pass and trav-

51

eled to the central refugee control center in Wurzburg, Germany.

Arriving in Wurzburg, Czech refugees were instructed to read many posted announcements. One announcement explained how to answer the questions of interrogators during the processing procedure. If the interrogator asked, "Why did you escape from Czechoslovakia?" We were to answer, "Because I am against Communism." This was a very important detail. The Communist regime of Czechoslovakia was a member of the United Nations, which in turn was providing relief for refugees all over Europe. If a refugee said they escaped because they were "against communism," they were accepted as a refugee. However, if an escapee said they were against the government of Czechoslovakia, then they would not be accepted as a refugee by the United Nations.

My first night in Wurzburg, I slept in a huge garage filled with old, creaky bunk beds. When people learned that a priest was among them, they started to visit my bunk. Some sought words of faith and encouragement. Others simply wanted to look at me, because they had never seen a priest so tired, dirty and unshaven. In fact, I looked just like they did! After a while, I had to pretend to be asleep when I saw people coming.

INTERROGATION

The first man to interrogate me was a young Lithuanian. He wanted to know why I escaped and what I had done in Czechoslovakia. I explained that I had no ID, but was a Catholic priest named Walter Marek. When I refused to tell him exactly what I had done as a priest, he got angry and took me over to the director of the control center.

The director was a nice Jewish man, who spoke several languages. We spoke in German and I told him some, but not all of what I had done in Czechoslovakia. He also was not satisfied with my answers and took me by jeep to the American secret police headquarters. The American headquarters were housed in the only building left standing on the public square of Wurzburg. The rest of downtown Wurzburg lay in ruin, littered with countless bomb craters and bullet holes.

At American headquarters, I was interrogated by two stern agents. Surprisingly, they knew that Father Walter Marek had escaped from Czechoslovakia, but they could not be sure that I was he. After about an hour of questioning one said, "If you get an ID from the Vatican, then we will be convinced you are Walter Marek." To this I replied, "I would not know where to write and I have no money for a stamp." The American agents conferred again, then suggested I visit the Catholic Bishop in Wurzburg. They called ahead for me and made an appointment for the next morning. Things were looking up.

In the morning, I borrowed some money and took a streetcar into the suburbs of Wurzburg. The Bishop's offices were located in an old monastery which was as quiet as a tomb. A young priest greeted me at the door and said I would meet first with the Vicar General. In a diocese, the Vicar is second in change. I got the distinct impression that everyone had been anxiously awaiting my arrival.

BISHOP DOEPFNER OF WURZBURG

The Vicar General was an elderly German priest. When I entered his office, he was sitting at his desk smoking a cigar. Demonstrating respect, I remained standing and spoke to him in German. I politely told him who I was, where I was from and what I needed from the Catholic Church. He looked up at me dismissively and said, "We have had bad experiences with the Czechs." This remark made me very angry indeed. For an instant, I wanted to jump right over his desk and slap him. I wanted to take him by the shoulders and tell him in very straight language, "We have had bad experiences with the Germans!"

Regaining my composure, I calmly answered, "Monsignor, es gibt schlechte und gute Leute uberall." (There are good and bad people everywhere). Upon hearing this, he mellowed and gestured for me to sit. He now spoke to me only in Latin, "So you say you are a Catholic priest from the diocese of Regina Gradecensis? Then tell me this..." For over an hour, the Vicar General questioned me on almost everything a Catholic priest has to know. He challenged me repeatedly, but I was up to the task.

He had obtained a reference book containing the history of my diocese in Czechoslovakia. He tried to confuse me on certain dates and on the sequence of our Bishops, but I knew it all perfectly. At some point I asked him to stop, because I was getting tired. He smiled and answered in German, "Let me take you to the Bishop."

We walked the silent corridors of the monastery and finally arriving at the Bishop's offices. The Vicar must have made the "O.K." sign behind my back, because the Bishop received me very cordially. Only 40 years old at the time, Bishop Doepfner was the youngest Bishop in Germany. We talked for about 20 minutes. Finally, he said, "Do not worry about a thing. I will call the American authorities and inform them that you are indeed Father Walter Marek." Upon leaving his office, Bishop Doepfner gave me 30 German marks and his personal address. We corresponded for many years after.

Feeling completely relieved, I traveled back to the refugee control center. When I arrived, everything had changed. Everyone was very polite to me and I was given a displaced persons identity card. A short time later, two students from Prague approached me and said that they had heard of me. Both spoke English, so I asked them if they knew of Mr. Sullivan, who had been the director of Catholic relief services in Prague. Imagine my surprise when one of the students replied, "Not only do I know Mr. Sullivan, I have his address and will write a letter to him on your behalf!" This most obvious blessing delighted me.

EICHSTÄTT, GERMANY

The following day, I traveled with some other Czechs to a refugee camp in the Bavarian town of Eichstätt. We were told that everything we needed would be at the Eichstätt camp. In reality, the camp was just an old barracks, recently abandoned by Jewish refugees in route to Israel. I managed to find a little room with a bedspring and slept there with my winter boots under my head.

The next morning, I started to learn about life in a refugee camp. The camp garbage dump contained piles of empty tin cans. I pick-up a few of the cans and cleaned them as best I could. I carried one can to the soup line, and filled another with water or coffee. Someone soon stole the cans from my little room. Five of us had to share one spoon. I looked after that spoon very carefully.

On my 4th day at Eichstätt, Father Petr Lekavy visited the camp. Of course, I knew of him from the Czech underground. He was now acting as Apostolic Delegate to the refugee camps. We spoke for about half and hour, then he commissioned me as the official priest of the camp. I was very happy to have work. I would earn about 100 Marks per month!

Delighted with my new commission, I quickly requested an audience with the local Bishop. The Bishop was very friendly to me and generally sympathetic to the plight of refugees. He said that he remembered me standing in the Cathedral during his sermon the Sunday before. That particular sermon had been very impressive. He described a miraculous event he'd witnessed during a recent visit to Lourdes, France.

Long lines of German POWs were being marched through the city of Lourdes. A Frenchman was standing on the sidewalk watching the POWs go by, when he suddenly recognized one of the Germans. This German had been a guard at the concentration camp where the Frenchman was held during the war. The Frenchman ran out to the former German guard and they looked at each other, then the two men embraced. For a few minutes, the line of POWs and everyone around stood still. The Bishop had witnessed this miracle

55

of forgiveness and shared it during his sermon. The entire congregation was moved to tears.

THE AFTERMATH OF MY ESCAPE

Our Parish in Litomyšl had the title of Provostship, because in the 14th century it was established as the Bishopric. During the Hussite wars the Bishop's see was destroyed and never renewed. Pastor Durek tried hard to restore the glory of the Parish, but Communist authorities always thwarted his efforts. If he had agreed to cooperate, then he would have been allowed to renew the Parish. He was not that kind of man.

Pastor Durek had frequently encouraged me to escape. He was brave and dreamed of escaping, but his age and fragile health prevented it. Someone told him that it was possible to escape by car into Germany. I was very skeptical of this plan, because it required driving across two long wood planks which had to be placed over a deep creek bed. If anything went wrong, we were sure to be caught. During our periodic visits to the springs of Marianske Lazne, near the eastern border of Germany, Pastor Durek would always joke, "Walter, keep an eye out for some long planks!"

I think Pastor Durek's true dream was to live in America. He had spent about 18 months there during 1920-1921. He spoke about the United States frequently and enthusiastically. On several occasions, he said my brightest future was in America. Being trapped inside Communist controlled Czechoslovakia, I guess I never took his remarks seriously. In time, I would see the wisdom in his words.

Pastor Durek suffered great consequences for my escape. He was arrested and convicted of collusion. As part of his sentence, Communist authorities banished him from Litomyšl for life. These facts still haunt me and I believe he died of a broke heart. I was never able to thank him for all that he had done for me. I do know that he was not bitter. He managed to send me one message in Germany. It read simply, "I envy you."

CHAPTER 5

REFUGEE PRIEST

Post-war Europe was a treacherous place. Some 10 million refugees were left in the wake of World War II. Jews that survived the Holocaust and people from English speaking countries were often put in charge of refugee camps, because they were educated and knew multiple languages. They worked as camp directors, field directors and regional directors. Like me, each of these people had a story of redemption and I made many friends in the refugee camps.

I was to live in Germany for about two years, working as a priest in four different refugee camps. Father Lekavy directed my work and I stayed at each camp for about 6 months. I found most native Germans and Sudeten Germans to be very understanding and helpful. Most Germans felt regret for the war and compensated by being especially sympathetic to the people it had displaced. Of course, many Germans were also displaced. I had countless joyful experiences in the camps and deeply enjoyed my work. How could I have known that God had even bigger plans for me?

HOW I MET BISHOP FRANCIS J. HAAS

As promised, the students from Prague sent a letter to Mr. Sullivan for me. It read in part, "I am here!" Mr. Sullivan tracked me down at Eichstätt, leaving a telephone message that he wished to see me. We corresponded and he sent me a rail ticket to Frankfort. When I arrived at the train station, he was waiting with a sign written in Czech, "Father Walter Marek." He also brought an interpreter, as he spoke only English and I did not. I mentioned that I was hungry and Mr. Sullivan graciously offered to buy me dinner.

We walked to a German restaurant that specialized in American cuisine. After we ordered Mr. Sullivan asked, "Father Marek, there is an American Bishop dining at the next table. He is very interested in the plight of refugees like you. Would you like to meet him?" The interpreter looked at me funny and said in Czech, "Say yes!" Indeed, Mr. Sullivan was referring to the Most Reverend Francis J. Haas from Grand Rapids, Michigan. Fortune had again smiled upon me, as Bishop Haas was visiting Frankfort for just one day. It is a miracle that we happened to be at the same restaurant.

The whole evening was wonderful. At some point Bishop Haas asked me, "Would you like to come to my diocese in America?" The Czech interpreter gave me that look again and said, "He likes you. Say yes!" The good Bishop gave me his calling card and promised to sponsor my immigration to The United States. This turned out to be one of the greatest meetings of my life.

EICHSTÄTT 1949

I lived in the Eichstätt refugee camp from spring to autumn of 1949. I had learned that life in a refugee camp was completely different from life at home, where one was sheltered and protected. In a refugee camp there were no laws or ordinances. Everyone had to live with what they had carried to the camp. Eventually, about 2000 people were housed in the Eichstätt barracks, called "Jagerkaserne." My task was to provide hope and organize religious events.

The local Bishop gave me permission to use a small church in town. He also gave me access to a church warehouse, which I found to contain beautiful old altars and all manner of useful paraphernalia. I was honored when the Bishop gave me his own chalice to use. I built a nice little chapel at the camp and gave daily devotions. Many of the refugees needed spiritual guidance. It felt very good to work as a priest again.

At a big camp meeting, I announced to the refugees that Sunday Mass would be held at the church in town. The camp administrator helped me. He stood on a chair and said, "People, go to the church and make the new priest happy. He is a nice guy." This must have worked, because nearly 100 refugees walked with me to the little church that Sunday! This scene impressed most of the local Germans, but a few had strong opinions against Czech refugees. There was a large contingent of displaced Sudeten Germans at the Eichstätt camp. Most of these people were forced to flee Sudetenland at the end of the war and many Czechs had helped to assure their departure. Even with the tables and the fates now turned, I never heard a Czech say to a Sudeten German, "See, now you are in the same situation as we are, refugees." Indeed, most Sudeten Germans I met were very cooperative and supportive of their Czech Brothers.

MORTAL DANGER AT EICHSTÄTT

It is not easy to write about the danger of being killed. I was once in mortal danger at Eichstätt and regrettably by my own people. Some Czech refugees disliked me, because I was openly sympathetic to Slovaks and supported an independent Slovak state. Today, the Slovaks have their own state, but at the time most Czechs were vehemently against Slovak independence and called them "Separatists." Eichstätt had about 300 Slovak and 1,700 Czech refugees. About 300 of the Czechs were young people without parents, money or work skills. These young Czechs had virtually no prospects for the future and they knew it. In this hopeless atmosphere, it was easy for a few Czech rabble-rousers to stir discontent and direct it toward Slovaks. Tensions were stretched to the breaking point when an older Slovak priest criticized Czech youths during a camp meeting.

The Czech-Slovak conflict at Eichstätt had more to do with pent-up frustration than anything else, but it escalated into a very dangerous situation. I received word that a group of young Czech men intended to kill the Slovak priest. Concerned for his life, I secretly met with him and told him of their plan. He was mortified and did not know what to do. I advised him to leave the camp immediately and go to France, where I knew he had friends. I offered

59

to give him 50 Marks to travel. He left for France the very next morning.

The Slovak priest's departure probably saved his life, but it infuriated the young Czechs. I now became the object of their hate. They were convinced that I was hiding the priest at the Bishop's palace in town. The young men confronted me and demanded that I bring him back to the camp. If I did not return the Slovak priest, they would kill me instead. These hopeless young men were terribly misguided.

I explained that the priest was not in hiding, but had gone to live with friends in France. Naturally, the Slovaks blamed the Czechs for their priest's departure and a riot soon erupted. I tried to stop the fighting, but knives were flashing and there was little I could do. American authorities resolved the situation by transferring all the Slovaks to another camp. I missed many of those people in the church choir as they had lovely voices.

In autumn 1949, word came that the Czech refugees at Eichstätt were to be transferred to a camp in Ulm. Many of the refugees wanted to take belongings to Ulm, such as little coal stoves and small furniture. The camp director prohibited this, saying that Ulm would have everything we needed. Of course, we'd heard that story before.

Being the priest, I was given a whole freight car to transport the altar, pews and other church materials. Some Czechs came to me and asked, "Can we put a few things in your car Father?" "Certainly," I said. We soon realized that we would need a plan to accomplish this feat, because the camp director was watching everyone closely. So, two pretty Czech girls went to talk to the director. While he was preoccupied, we loaded a pile of belongings into my freight car, right behind his back! Soon, we were on the way to Ulm, Germany.

THE ULM REFUGEE CAMP

I learned important lessons at Eichstätt, which were to serve me well throughout my tenure in the refugee camps. Priests usually stay at a church and serve a certain congregation for several years. In the refugee camps, I was surrounded by many different nationalities and religions. I had to learn how to be flexible, without becoming entangled in the politics or beliefs of any group. Once in Ulm, I was able to establish my own church pretty quickly. Most of the Czech families came to like me and attendance was usually good at Sunday Mass.

WORKING WITH THE AMERICAN CIC

Once established in Ulm, an American agent quietly invited me to work with the Counter Intelligence Corps (CIC). Perhaps the CIC knew of my experience in the Czech underground. I must admit that I have always enjoyed intelligence work. At one time, I even entertained thoughts of working for the Vatican information center. My CIC contact was called "Mr. Pocket." He took me to CIC headquarters one night to meet the station head, Mr. Beyer.

Mr. Beyer seemed glad to meet me and asked for some information. He wanted to know about a Czech named Mr. Schulz, who was the chief administrator for about 2000 Czech refugees. Specifically, Mr. Beyer wanted to know if Mr. Schulz was a Jew. This was very surprising to me, so I him asked jokingly, "If Mr. Schultz is a Jew, would that be good or bad for him?" Mr. Beyer smiled and replied, "My name is Beyer and I am definitely a Jew!" We parted amicably and I performed several investigations for the CIC.

Something had bothered me about the Mr. Shultz question. In Litomyšl, a rumor persisted that some 10 Communist informants lived in town. One of the rumored informants was the sister of Mr. Schulz. I had never met this woman, but her husband was a very good violinist who played in my church orchestra. Mr. Schulz proved to be a good man and after his term as camp administrator, he became a successful businessman in Germany. We always got along very well.

THE PFORZHEIM REFUGEE CAMP

I was not pleased when Father Lekavy assigned me to the refugee camp in Pforzheim, Germany. I called his office with intentions of turning down the commission. Upon hearing this his assistant said, "Walter, you are the only person who has managed to stay on Petr's good side. Take my advice and take the commission." I decided to follow her advice.

Pforzheim was in the French section of interest after the war. The camp barracks were on a hill overlooking the entire city. The view was good, but the sight was terrible. Pforzheim was in complete ruin and one couldn't help but wonder why? I heard two explanations, but I don't know why the city was destroyed.

The first story was that the Nazis had been developing an atom bomb in Pforzheim and a rocket that could carry it to Washington D.C.. To halt the project, Allied bombers had leveled the entire city. The second story seemed slightly more plausible. An American plane had been shot down over Pforzheim and its pilots managed to parachute into the nearby forest. Local Germans had captured the pilots and alerted Nazi authorities. After being beaten by the Gestapo, the doomed airmen were taken the city square and publicly hanged. As the first pilot was hung, the second was able to use a small radio to alert London of his fate. Allied bombers had leveled Pforzheim the very next day.

A GERMAN PRIEST IN PFORZHEIM

By the time I arrived in Pforzheim, I had learned much about being a refugee priest. I understood the practical importance of working with other priests in the area. In this spirit, I invited a German priest from Pforzheim to be the main speaker at one of our special camp programs. The German priest was happy to oblige. Six nationalities attended the program and he spoke very well to all of us.

He returned the kindness by inviting me to Sunday Mass at his church. It was a very impressive ceremony with a celebration in the afternoon. His church was brand new, having been destroyed by bombs and rebuilt in a modern style from concrete. Many steps lead to the main alter. Upon these steps, he had the alter boys sit in a special formation.

Before Mass, some fifty alter boys were dressing in the basement of the church. Being boys, they made a great racket and laughed so loudly that we could hear them up in the sacristy. People seated in the church also heard them. The priest became furious and called the boys to the sacristy. They appeared in the doorway, still laughing and talking. Without warning, the priest greeted each boy with a hearty slap across the face. That is a sight I have never forgotten.

THE TRAUNSTEIN REFUGEE CAMP

When people at Traunstein heard that I was going to America, I became quite famous. Very few Czechs had been able to go to America. In order to be eligible, they had to prove that they had crossed the border into Germany before midnight on December 31, 1948. Luckily, my situation made me exempt from that particular rule. I still had to obtain a special visa, which was granted only to artists, clergy and employees of the American government.

Several refugees came to me and offered advice. I wondered how these people had acquired such information. For example, a young man came to me and said, "Father, if you are not getting a salary, go then to the German unemployment office and you can draw some money." I did not know that the German government was paying wages in the refugee camps. Another person came and said, "Father, when you leave Germany, you are entitled to a refund of the religious tax you've paid over the past two years, because you are not a German citizen."

The advice of a Czech surprised me to no end. He said, "Your ticket from Hamburg to New York can be changed to Le Havre, France right on the ship. If you make this change you will get a refund of $15.00!" I decided to try this advice, as the extra money would come in very handy. As usual, the Czech was right and I got back $15.00 on my $200.00 ticket. I also got the opportunity to see Paris, which I still treasure.

My father had dreamed of seeing Paris, but was never able. When I arrived in Paris, there was a general strike and none of the public transportation was moving. The travel agency arranged a bus trip, which took us through the French countryside to the port of Le Havre. It was most beautiful.

The European economy was still in shambles. Young Jews worked on street corners in most large cities, buying and selling whatever they could. They specialized in changing money. Before leaving France, I went to a Jewish man on a street corner and told him that I was going to America and would require US dollars. I gave the Jew about 1,000 German Marks. He made the calculations and gave me about $300.00. This was the money I carried to America.

CHAPTER 6

SOCIAL REVOLUTION

I think it is appropriate to speak now to the students and parents of students who are reading. History teaches us that university students are often on the cutting-edge of social change in a country. Sure, students become the professors, doctors, lawyers, teachers and leaders of a nation. However, the cultural climate of a university informs students with a unique sense of social justice, which they often carry throughout life. During the European Revolutions of 1848, student revolts had a great impact on the futures of many countries. For better or worse, this can also be said for the Czech university students who protested Nazi occupation in 1939.

Between 1918 and 1939, Prague had separate universities for German and Czech students. As Nazi influence grew in Sudetenland and elsewhere in our country, these universities became bitter rivals. Czech students were among the first to realize the Nazi's true intentions. At one point, German students stole the insignia flags from the Czech University. Today, this may seem like a harmless prank, but in those days it was an act national humiliation. The incident resulted in grim confrontations between Czech and German university students. One of my former Gymnasium classmates named Zenger, told me how such events lead to the Czech student uprising in 1939. He was among the students imprisoned at Oranienburg. We met by chance in a refugee camp after the war.

Czech culture always prized intellectuals, especially those we called "Polyhistors." In my youth, a Polyhistor was someone who knew everything there was to know. In 1939, Hitler wisely stopped the flow of Czech university students. His terrible vision for Czechoslovakia could not be realized if well-educated Czechs continued to pour forth from Prague. He also muted the influence of existing Czech Intelligentsia. Many brilliant Czechs suffered terribly under both the Nazi and Communist occupations. I have known two Polyhistors and both ended up Communist prisoners, forced into menial labor.

THE VELVET REVOLUTION

University students in Prague made the Velvet Revolution a success. The "Sametová Revoluce", occurred between mid-November and the end of December 1989. It all began with a peaceful student demonstration in Prague, which was violently suppressed by Communist authorities. This time the violence shown by the Communist regime was more than the Czech people could bear. Overnight, new demonstrations emerged and by November 20, 1989 some 500,000 Czechs protested non-violently against the Communists. On November 27th Czechs held a national strike, which brought the entire nation to a standstill. On November 28, 1989 the Communist Party relinquished control, setting the stage for free elections! I shed many tears on that day.

One of my relatives participated in the Velvet Revolution. Now a judge, he was then among the student protestors. He told me that the Velvet Revolution succeeded for one simple reason. Though Communist Party members, the parents of students chose not to alert Communist authorities of the protest. Many earlier student protest movements had been betrayed by parents. Unfettered by loyal parents, the Czech students in Prague lead social change and the Velvet Revolution succeeded. The era of Communist rule in Czechoslovakia was over.

BILL CLINTON IN PRAGUE

The Communist regime in Czechoslovakia lasted from February 1948 to November 1989. During this period, university admission was not based on a student's intellectual talent. If your parents didn't belong to the Communist Party, then you were simply ineligible for university study. In this way, the Communists prayed upon well-meaning Czech families. Many joined the Party just to ensure a college education for their children.

Many, many non-Communist students applied to universities only to be rejected on political grounds. Predictably, the Communist Party policy on higher education eventually resulted in a constipated and intellectually stifling university system. As a result, rich and powerful Communist Party members often sent their children abroad to study. One such student, Jan Kopold, was a roommate of Bill Clinton at Oxford. Jan's maternal grandparents were founding members of the Czech Communist Party.

Naturally, the Czech and Bill Clinton became good friends. Jan accompanied Bill Clinton on his controversial trip to Moscow in 1969. During that trip, the future president also visited the Kopold family in Prague. Bill Clinton's visit apparently left a great impression on the Kopolds. Jan's father, Bedrich, reportedly told the future President, "Perhaps someday you will return to Prague as an American Ambassador."

It seems that the Kopolds also left a great impression on young Bill Clinton. In early 1994, President Bill Clinton visited Prague to meet with Visegrad leaders. During this visit he stopped-in on the Kopold family, telling the press they were, "old friends I have long admired." Jan Kopold had died in Turkey in 1970, but his father and mother welcomed President Clinton. Much has been said of Bill Clinton's relationship to the Kopold family, because they were known members of the Communist Party. I believe Mr. Clinton simply remembered and appreciated the words Bedrich had said to him in 1969. He did return to Prague as an American Ambassador, but with the title of President of The United States.

DENIED STUDY, VÁCLAV HAVEL BECOMES PRESIDENT

After the Velvet Revolution, the Czech people demonstrated their cultural appreciation for intellectuals and artists by electing Václav

Havel President of Czechoslovakia. He is the only man to be both President of Czechoslovakia and President of the Czech Republic. His story is very interesting, but I will cover just a little.

Václav Havel came from a family of brilliant Czechs who were not Communist Party members. Though he showed terrific promise as a student and leader, Václav was not allowed to attend a university. However, his mind could not be suppressed and he became a political activist and playwright.

Naturally, the Communists imprisoned him numerous times, once for a period of 4 years. He responded by writing a powerful play and many essays while imprisoned. He later became leader of the Civic Forum, a political party created soon after the Velvet Revolution. When the Communists relinquished control in November 1989, it was none other than Václav Havel who was elected President of Czechoslovakia in December. Of course, President Clinton visited President Havel in 1994. Another amazing Czech story!

Even before becoming president, Václav Havel was much loved by most Czechs. Due to his political activism, the Communist police watched him day and night, following him everywhere he went. On one occasion, he and his wife Olga were traveling somewhere and got lost. The Communist police, who usually remained invisible, pulled him over and said, "Václav, you are going the wrong way. Follow us!"

THE BRIDGE OF INTELLIGENTSIA

Each generation of university students reinforces a nation's foundation of intelligentsia. In Prague, we have a living memorial to the suppression of intelligentsia. It is a bridge built by imprisoned doctors, priests, professors and other intellectuals. These remarkable individuals were forced to work by mindless guards and tortured if disobedient. One must wonder what they might have accomplished, had they not been forced into bridge building? Today, this bridge is called, "The Bridge of Intelligentsia."

Whenever I can, I tell Czech people to learn German and realize that as neighbors we must cooperate. The border and relations between us must be open and sincere. Before the war, over 80% of all Czechoslovakian business was with Germany. It's imperative to do the same today. Germany is a big country at the center of Europe. Transportation is very easy between the neighbors. As always, communication and economics are the keys to freedom and peace.

CHAPTER 7

INTO THE ARMS OF AMERICA

When I visit my memories of Europe, I am often filled with old but familiar feelings. My young life was full of challenges, complications and dire uncertainty. By the grace of God, each challenge turned into good fortune. With faith all things are possible.

I was a sickly child, but at the Gymnasium in Prague the Jesuits made me into a good athlete. I exercised very hard and at age 15, I won the 60-meter sprint at the Prague stadium. Coincidently, I met James "Ted" Meredith on the very same day in 1933.

Ted Meredith was the very first American I ever met. He had won 2 gold medals at the 1912 Olympics, which were held in Stockholm, Sweden. I remember being very impressed by this American Olympian. He was very tall. On that day, I could never have imagined that the greatest challenges and greatest fortunes of my life would be in The United States of America.

BISHOP HASS WRITES THE AMERICAN CONSULATE

Bishop Haas wrote a letter to the American Consulate saying he would sponsor my immigration to America. His letter stated that my salary would be $400.00 a year with the possibility of an additional $400.00 from other sources. I would be assigned to Empire, Michigan. This last fact became worrisome. I checked several maps of Michigan and Empire was not on any of them! However, the American Consulate said my papers were in order and my visa was granted. Bishop Haas sent me my ticket to America.

The reality of going to America was a little frightening. This was not a vacation. My life in Germany had been relatively good and I enjoyed working in the camps. The work was fulfilling. Nevertheless, I honored the sponsorship of Bishop Francis Haas.

TO ELLIS ISLAND ON THE S.S. WASHINGTON

I was already 32 years old when I came to America. The little English I spoke had been learned in the refugee camps. After the bus ride to Le Havre, I boarded the S.S. Washington, which would take me to America. On that day she was moored next to France's great ocean liner the Ile de France, which I later learned had the first ocean going, consecrated Roman Catholic chapel.

The most dramatic moment of my life was when the S.S. Washington pulled away from the dock at Le Havre and the gap between the land and the ship was getting bigger and bigger. I had butterflies in my stomach. I wondered, shall I ever return to Europe? What will be my destiny now?

Pastor Durek had sparked my interest in America. I remembered how enthusiastically he spoke of his visit. He had traveled from New York to Chicago to Texas, visiting the Czech Parishes. He told us all about the fast trains, organized crime in Chicago, prohibition and life in the Catholic Church in America. As the ship turned to the west, I thought of him and smiled. He would be proud to see me now.

POST-WAR PRIEST IMMIGRATION

After the war, refugees from Europe immigrated to places all over the world. Refugee priests went to wherever and whoever would take them. In the United States, the Catholic Church published a list of dioceses that would accept refugee priests. Of the 150 dioceses in America, about 30 would not accept a refugee priest. Another 30 dioceses were undecided on the matter. The remaining 90 dioceses welcomed foreign refugee priests. Naturally, dioceses were very selective about refugee priests. For example, the diocese in Fargo, North Dakota was especially interested in having Father Petr Lekavy and a few other influential priests.

Father Petr Lekavy was a very talented man, but he was also

prone to angry outbursts and could be argumentative. In my interactions with him, I found him to be a man of clear vision and straight talk. Such men are often misunderstood. The Vatican must have received complaints about him, because he often told priests not to go to Rome. He once told me, "Walter, they don't want us in Rome, we are refugees!" Later someone told me, "Do you know why he didn't want you to go to Rome? Because he was afraid Vatican officials would ask you about him."

During and after the war, Father Lekavy had information from all sources. He was a very good politician. In Czechoslovakia, he had been the Vice Mayor of Brno for the Popular Party. Brno is the capital of Moravia and the second largest city in the Czech Republic. Father Lekavy immigrated to America in the 1950's and continued his distinguished career in the Catholic Church.

ARRIVING IN AMERICA

I arrived on Ellis Island on March 31, 1951, after an 8-day voyage. On Ellis Island, the aunt of some friends I'd made at Eichstätt met me. They too were waiting to come to America and had arranged for this wonderful woman to greet me. She was a great character who spoke several languages and talked of experiences she'd had all over the world.

As a younger woman she had worked as an American IRS agent on ships traveling from Europe to the U.S. Her job was to get friendly with the ladies on the ship and learn who had bought expensive jewelry. Naturally, most of the rich ladies were eager to display their fine new jewelry. She informed customs officials and the agents waited for the ladies to declare their jewelry. If they did not declare, then they were in much trouble! She also told me that she no longer went to church. It seems that on one occasion she had placed 25 cents in the collection tray only to have the usher give it back to her.

I enjoyed New York immensely and almost didn't make it to Michigan. The woman took me to the office of her boss Mr. Brandt, which was on Broadway. Sitting in the office, I witnessed something absolutely unknown of in Europe. Two young film agents from Hollywood came in and took off their overcoats. Each then proceeded to roll his coat into a tight ball and place it next him on the bench. I had never seen anything like that. In Europe we hung our coats on a rack! I talked to the men briefly, using the rough English I'd learned in the refugee camps. They were interested in my story, but never made a movie about me.

Mr. Brandt was a wealthy Jew who owned several movie houses in New York and by chance had a cottage in Michigan. He took a liking to me and made a generous offer. He encouraged me to stay in New York. He said that he knew Cardinal Spellman personally. With one telephone call, he could make a deal for me to stay in town.

I thanked him for his offer, but declined. I had made a commitment to Bishop Haas and was determined to fulfill it. Some people in New York looked upon Michigan like it was at the very end of the Earth. Someone told me that living in Michigan had only one advantage; I could buy a cheap car there!

FIRST MASS IN AMERICA

My first impression of the American Catholic Church was very favorable. I said Mass in Latin on Long Island in a very large church after Easter. To my amazement, the church was full of school-aged children. The girls were on my left and boys on my right, about one thousand each. The girls all wore very fine Easter bonnets, the quality of which I'd never seen before. The boys were also dressed in fine cloths.

The young priest gave an excellent sermon. I later found that particular sermon in a book of English sermons, which I'd bought shortly after arriving in America. I could never give a sermon from a book. I read many written sermons for inspiration, but my sermons had to be from my heart and contain my own thoughts and insight.

BY TRAIN TO GRAND RAPIDS, MICHIGAN

Bidding my New York friends farewell, I boarded a train that would take me to the end of the Earth. Luckily, the trip only took about 2 days and I enjoyed seeing some of America by rail. When I pulled into Grand Rapids, Michigan, Bishop Haas was there to greet me.

The next day we traveled to Sacred Heart Parish in Muskegon Heights, where Bishop Haas appointed me Second Assistant to Pastor Albert Kehren. Pastor Kehren's First Assistant was Father Eugene Van Bergen. Both men were jovial and talkative. They were to have a very great influence on my development as an American.

Upon leaving Bishop Haas said to me, "Father, I hope you will not be preferential to the Slovak people here." I assured him that I would serve all parishioners of all nationalities equally, just as I had in the refugee camps.

CHAPTER 8

PRIESTHOOD

EIGHTEEN MONTHS IN MUSKEGON HEIGHTS

Naturally, I tried to be very respectful of everyone in my new country. Twice I made inappropriate remarks, which were never really accepted and thankfully taken only as jokes. One beautiful morning, I was walking along the sidewalk while parents brought their children to school in cars. I noticed that the air was suddenly full of exhaust fumes. When I mentioned this observation to my colleagues at breakfast, it was very clear that no one but me considered it a danger!

Another time, I was observing the situation of public schools and their teachers. "Is that all you pay the teachers?" I asked. "Be quiet," I was told, "or our taxes will go up!" In the 1950's, American teachers had to find jobs in the summer time and students used to say, "Let's find the gas station jobs, before the teachers get them!"

Despite incidents when it would have been better if I'd kept my mouth shut, I was appointed Spiritual Leader of the Junior Legion of Mary, which in our parish had about 15 girls. The girls wanted to honor my 33rd birthday, which had been an important age for Jesus and ordered for me a cake. They told the baker to write "Happy Birthday Father" on the cake. We all laughed heartily when they opened the box and the cake read, "Happy Birthday Daddy!"

Life in America was a bunch of interesting surprises. I attended parish festivals, picnics, dinners, priest gatherings, dinner meetings with the Bond Club of the Parish and had countless new experiences. I also made many mistakes, not only in English grammar, but also in life. I always made-up for my shortcommings by playing piano. I routinely entertained the 13 classrooms of our Parish school and the Parish societies at their meetings. Eighteen months went by very quickly at Sacred Heart when suddenly, both

Father Van Bergen and I were sent to other Parishes.

One great experience I had at Sacred Heart was attending the Congress of Slovak Catholic Organizations in America. The Congress was held in our Parish, as there were many Slovak families in Muskegon Heights. Slovak leaders came from all over the U.S. to talk, celebrate and conduct elections. Being a Czech Catholic Priest, I felt right at home. One evening, when the spirit was high, I played all the Slovak songs I knew. The whole congregation (about 500) sang with me and enjoyed themselves immensely. Since my childhood, I have been for Slovak independence.

FIVE YEARS IN TRAVERSE CITY

In autumn 1952, I was transferred to Traverse City to work with Pastor Russell Passeno. Father Passeno was a great musician. He could have easily been a professional pianist and was an excellent conductor of the church choir. We often played music together, I on the violin and he on piano. During the summertime, he visited Interlochen Music Camp almost every night.

Interlochen was named after a place in Switzerland called "Interlacken" meaning, "Place between two lakes." Founded in 1928 by Dr. Joseph Maddy, the beautiful camp lies between Green Lake and Duck Lake. In early years, Dr. Maddy often conducted The World Youth Orchestra on Sunday nights. This was the very best youth orchestra of its time. On the first Sunday of each concert season, when the students had had few rehearsals, they performed Dvorak's Symphony Number 8. Today, all Interlochen concert performances conclude with a theme from Howard Hansen's "Romantic" Symphony. Needless to say, I love Interlochen.

Besides Interlochen, I enjoyed Sunday afternoon performances of the High School Symphonic Band, conducted by Professor Wilson. Before coming to Traverse City, I had heard symphonic bands on only two occasions, both of which were associated with the war. Both the Germans and the Communists had arrived in

Czechoslovakia with good symphonic bands. However, in Traverse City I was able to really listen and absorb the sounds the band. My great love of music would find exciting new outlets in America.

THREE GREAT COMPOSERS

The first composer I ever met was a Czech named Joseph Bohuslav Foerster. Our music professor at the Gymnasium dedicated an entire performance to his works and I sang in the choir. We were delighted when Mr. Foerster sent word that he would attend our performance. After the performance, he congratulated our work and talked to several choir members. I was one the boys he talked to.

During my time in Traverse City, Interlochen sponsored the International Congress of National Songs. I asked the event organizers if a Czechoslovakian composer was attending? They were unsure and admitted that they were having trouble reading the attendee applications. The applications had been completed in English, but the organizers couldn't tell if names were of men or women. They didn't want to pair people inappropriately. One organizer pointed to an application and asked, "Father, is this the name of a man or a woman?" Everyone laughed when I replied, "Neither. It is the name of a building in Prague!" After struggling to improve my English, it was nice to be of use as an interpreter.

Many great composers attended the International Congress at Interlochen and I was fortunate enough to meet two of them. I met the famous Hungarian composer named Koralyi. By this time he was over 80 years old, but still very energetic and gracious. Naturally, he introduced me to his beautiful young wife. After his death, Mrs. Koralyi looked after his music and legacy.

I also met the Russian composer, Dmitry Borisovich Kabalevsky. I remember going to his room for a visit. He was closely guarded by two Communist police officers. They were very suspicious of me, probably fearing that Mr. Kabalevsky planned to defect to America. I paid them no attention and said, "Mr. Kabalevsky, I am Czech and I welcome you to the United States." His eyes spoke to me first, then he said, "Czech, thank you very, very much." When I bid him farewell, the two officers walked me to the door, each still giving me very suspicious looks.

My time with Father Russell Passeno came to a close when I received an appointment to St. Simon Parish in Ludington, Michigan. I was to serve as First Assistant to Pastor Raymond Drinan. Father Drinan had a completely different personality, having served 23 years as a chaplain in the US Navy. He was stationed in China during World War II and was head chaplain for the whole Pacific theatre. He was in Honolulu when Pearl Harbor was attacked and told me about the experience. Father Drinan had many stories to tell.

SIX MONTHS IN LUDINGTON

Father Drinan loved to tell the story of a Saturday afternoon confession period he once scheduled for sailors on a ship. As I write, I'm inclined to correct my English. Until meeting Father Drinan, I commonly used words like "boat" or "ship." "Excuse me," he'd always say, "It was not a ship. It was a vessel!" Anyway, his scheduled confession periods never got much attendance. Except for one particular Saturday when sailor after sailor came down the steps to the Confessional. Father Drinan wondered why so many men were suddenly coming to confession. He climbed the stairs to investigate. He saw a sergeant asking every sailor that went by, "Are you a Catholic?" If the man said yes, then the sergeant pushed him down the steps toward the Confessional. That is one way to do it!

Father Drinan was able to add a story about me to his catalogue. One Saturday I had a wedding ceremony to perform, which was all rehearsed and ready to go. I was surprised when the father of the bride came to the sacristy with a worried look on his face. He was concerned because the organist had not arrived. I told him not to worry; I would play the organ for them. I said, "When you hear the sound of the organ, walk down the aisle as we rehearsed."

I held the wedding up for a few minutes looking for the power switch on the organ, which I'd never played before. After performing a beautiful wedding march, I stepped down from the choir loft and calmly performed the ceremony. Upon finishing the wedding ceremony, I said to the smiling couple, "Please wait for the recession march." With this, I went back to the organ and played for the now laughing wedding party.

I was only with Father Drinan for 6 months, but I felt that he had made a man out of me. As it turned out, I would need that stamina and self-control for my next appointment. Evidently, my new Pastor had had some difficulty with previous assistants and was not looking forward to my arrival.

FIVE YEARS IN HASTINGS

My first meeting with the Pastor in Hastings was shocking and downright nasty. At the time, I remembered what some priests in Europe had told me. "You will find the Catholic Church in America too strict." At first I cried, but then I retaliated in a subtle way, which could make life rather impossible for he and his housekeeper.

He soon realized his mistake and told me to, "take it easy." Once reconciled, we became good friends. He had me straighten-out his personal finances and the finances of the parish. He later recommended me to Bishop Babcock in Grand Rapids, telling him, "You can give any appointment to Father Marek and he will do a good job." Once again, my early education in finance and accounting had come in handy.

MY HEART LIES IN A PARISH

I enjoyed my work as an Assistant and learned much. However, life in the United States could also be difficult for an immigrant who

79

was nearing middle age. I always had to live in small rooms and obey the rules of each house. Between 1951 and 1963, I sometimes felt like an unnecessary person. This all changed when I finally became a Pastor at the age of 45.

When I came to America, my chances of becoming the Pastor of a parish were slim. In those days, the American Catholic Church had an abundance of priests. However, knowing the history of the Catholic Church in Czechoslovakia after World War I, I began to see some similarities. I remember discussing the topic with a priest from Lithuanian. I said to him, "Just wait, they will beg us to take parishes one day!" This prediction turned out to be correct.

When Bishop Haas died in 1953, The Most Reverend Bishop Allen J. Babcock succeeded him. I always honored and respected the Bishops I met in Europe and America. Bishop Babcock began a sweeping diocesan collection, which succeeded even without support from some Pastors. He engaged the skill of many people with influence and money to assure the success of his vision. When I met Bishop Babcock, I knew my whole future would pivot on his words.

SEVEN YEARS IN LAKEWOOD CLUB

Bishop Babcock welcomed me cordially into his Grand Rapids office. He said, "Father, I have something for you. A Chaplaincy at Mercy Hospital in Muskegon has become available." He could see that I was not too happy with that appointment. After a short pause, he continued, "I will also make you Pastor of the nearby Church and you will enjoy double salary." Each position paid $100.00 a month. My room and board was included at the hospital. I eagerly accepted the two positions. I thanked Bishop Babcock, kissing his ring as was customary in Czechoslovakia.

My apartment at the hospital was on the 1st floor, isolated from the areas patients normally occupied. Several days before arriving at the hospital, I had my baby grand piano delivered to my quarters. This worried the Reverend Sisters a little, but they soon accepted my piano and me. Music creates all kinds of situations and fits into every mood. One day I was playing a little fast music. A Painter who was working down the hall came to my door and said, "Father, please do not play so fast, I cannot keep up with you!"

The Nuns who owned Mercy Hospital considered my job there to be my top priority, but I was easily able to balance both positions. Life as the Chaplain of a hospital was never considered by clergy to be very interesting. Actually, it was looked upon as one of the lowest appointments and often held by very old priests. One of the nurses asked me, "Why are you here? You are young and almost normal." When the hospital received a new and younger Nun as administrator, things were a little rough between us. In time, we worked together well.

SAINT MARY OF THE WOODS

I was elated when Bishop Babcock appointed me Pastor of my own Parish. My heart filled with joy, just as it had so many years before at Eichstätt. My Parish was in the community of Lakewood Club, which was not yet registered and as such not on the state map. At that time, the parish was commonly referred to as the "Mission of Montague."

Interestingly, Father Passeno had been the first Pastor of Montague. He built the church and developed the parish. The church was in a natural setting and had nice architecture, but the site was in very bad shape when I arrived. Three of my former Pastors had also spent time at Montague. It seemed that everyone had a story about the people of Lakewood Club. Some of the stories were funny and some were not. I had a story of my own before I ever saw the church!

I had not yet left Hastings, when a woman came to me about Montague. She said, "Father, my brother lives in your new Parish. The last time my daughter and I visited the church, she had to go to the bathroom outside! I hope you will install a new toilet." After my first Sunday mass, I told the congregation about this problem. The following Sunday, a parishioner from Chicago brought us a brand new commode.

The summer residents of Lakewood Club made a great difference in church attendance. The church was small, so I often gave two Masses in the summertime. Things were improving in the Parish, but for some reason a few of the local people didn't like the progress. When my new janitor, Sexton, put a beautiful lawn around the church (supposedly the first and only such lawn in the village), some vandals drove a car over the grass. Someone informed me that the vandals had been riding in a Jeep. If this person knew it was a Jeep, then they must have known who had done it!

The Parish grew from a few parishioners to over 150 families. One time, somebody tried to steal the Tabernacle with the Blessed Sacrament in it. They worked it over well, but could not open it. It was like a safe.

The third and nastiest act of vandalism happened when I acquired and furnished a Parish house. We finally had a nice meeting room, a kitchen and a place for the parish offices. I was very proud of the house. Shortly after we furnished the house, vandals broke-in and relieved themselves on our new couch.

Another problem developed when I installed a telephone in our new offices. In those days, telephone lines were usually shared. Several people accused me of stealing the line, saying that it was supposed to have gone to a local hall. Even with these problems, I never lost my love for the people. I guessed that the acts of vandalism had been done by a very few. I never showed any animosity toward the vandals, which probably disappointed them greatly.

When the residents of Lakewood Club sought to officially register the village, a group of community leaders asked me to go with them to the judge in Muskegon. I was happy to oblige. The judge listened to the opposing Township Supervisor, but said to him, "These people even brought their priest. They want to be independent." The judge granted our request. Later that year, a summer parishioner showed me a new map of Michigan and proudly pointed to the village of Lakewood Club. We were now on the map!

THE STORY OF BLUE LAKE FINE ARTS CAMP

One day a lady came to my door and asked who was playing the piano. I recognized her as a hospital volunteer who delivered books to our patients. She introduced herself and said that she played flute and was taking cello lessons from Mr. Gilbert Stansell. She expressed concern that I did not have many friends and suggested a soirée in her home. She would introduce me to Mr. Stansell and her husband who she said was an excellent pianist.

I was delighted and accepted her generous offer. As the day approached, I became increasingly excited to play with other musicians. After dinner that evening, we had a very fine session. Her husband played piano, she the flute, Mr. Stansell the cello and I the violin. The Stansells told me they were looking for a place to start a music camp. Mrs. Stansell said they had found a possible location on Lake Michigan. I was delighted to have some musical friends, especially friends who wanted to organize a music camp!

At our second soirée, Mrs. Stansell surprised me by saying that they had found an old deserted camp in my Parish area. Shortly after, she told me that a group of music teachers in Muskegon had put together $15,000 toward the purchase the old camp. When I learned that the treasurer for the group had no business experience, I immediately volunteered for the job. Things were developing quickly, but we still needed another $20,000.00 to make the purchase.

No bank in Muskegon was willing to take a chance and loan us the money. Finally, through some influence, the Lumberman's Bank in Muskegon agreed to loan us $20,000.00, provided 20 people would sign to secure the loan. The loan officer assumed all priests were poor, so he would not accept me as a signatory. I was disappointed, but soon found a doctor friend at the hospital who would sign in my place.

The old camp was located in Blue Lake Township, right on Little Blue Lake. It was only a mile or so from St. Mary of the Woods. We officially named our camp, "Blue Lake Fine Arts Camp." William Fritz Stansell, the Stansell's eldest son, became Blue Lake's first President. Fritz was a great President, who also taught music at the High School and the Community College in Muskegon.

Thus we started our little music camp. None of use could have imagined that Blue Lake would become the largest camp of its kind in the world, celebrating over 40 years of existence and serving about 6,000 students each summer. As a refugee priest from Czechoslovakia, it has been a great honor to act as Treasurer of Blue Lake Fine Arts Camp. I retain that position today.

My life in America had taken me in many new and exciting directions. I always tried to fulfill my obligations and enhance them with music, art and religion, which has always been most precious to me. With the leadership of the Stansell family and their high moral standards, Blue Lake has provided thousands of young art students with an excellent experience. After 7 years in Lakewood Club, the time came for me to move on. I was on my way to Frankfort, Michigan.

FOUR YEARS IN FRANKFORT

Bishop Babcock died in 1969 and with him my application for incardination into the Grand Rapids diocese. I was still officially a member of my diocese in Czechoslovakia. For a transfer I would need permission from the Vatican. My situation got brighter when the Bishop pro temp called me and asked if I would take a Parish in Frankfort, Michigan. He gave me his reasons and then said, "You will have to be in Frankfort tomorrow." He promised to send all my belongings, including my piano, to Frankfort as soon as possible. I was delighted with this new appointment and I consider my years in Frankfort the premium time of my life.

Frankfort is on the shore of Lake Michigan and attracts

thousands of tourists in the summertime. On Summer Sundays, the church of St. Ann often hosted 1000 additional people from all over the United States. It was a truly wonderful Parish.

The diocese of Grand Rapids was made smaller and Frankfort became part of the new diocese in Gaylord, Michigan. It was very exiting to be a part of a new diocese. Our first Bishop, Th.D. Edmund Szoka, was very successful in establishing the new diocese, both spiritually and financially.

FIVE YEARS IN KLACKING CREEK

Perhaps Bishop Szoka had been informed that I was a good man for cleaning-up and fixing the broken relationships in Parishes. One day he called me in Frankfort and said, "Walter, I need you in the Parish of Holy Family in Klacking Creek, near West Branch. If you take this appointment for me, I will never forget it!" I think he was pleased and a little surprised when I readily accepted. His advice? "Please, don't lose your smile over there."

Holy Family was located in the country and had a beautiful natural setting. Unfortunately, the premises had been long neglected and were in shambles. I got right to work. My janitor removed 23 loads of refuse in his pickup truck during the cleanup process. I thought he had taken the refuse to a dump, but when I visited his home on one occasion, I noticed the trash piled-up behind his house! In time, Holy Family came to look very nice and local people admired my work.

I have to admit that sometimes I was lonely at this isolated and relatively quiet Parish. In these moments, I remembered the words of our Bishop in Czechoslovakia, who emphasized that we must not be overcome by loneliness. He said, "You cannot run to your Mama. You have to stay with your people. You may be in the gravest danger or bound by snow in the mountains for weeks, but do not despair." This was very good advice and it has echoed through my life.

On Sunday afternoons, after everyone had left the church, I had to find ways of keeping myself occupied. One day, I returned to the church to find a young boy praying fervently at the side alter. At first I was quite impressed, but soon I noticed that his angelic face kept turning toward the Poor Box, which always contained some change on Sundays.

When that situation was resolved, I decided to take some refuse, along with a six-pack of beer to the dump. I met there a man who took the refuse and we shared some beer. He was very pleasant to talk to. I then drove to the local hospital and visited some of the tragically disabled people there. Seeing and talking to those less fortunate was always the best cure for my loneliness.

DON'T SHOOT! I'M A PRIEST

One incident from Klacking Creek has stood out in my mind for years. On a Sunday afternoon, a Parishioner called me and asked if I would go to the sheriff's office in West Branch. His son had been jailed there for killing a friend during an argument over a woman. The incident had happened just the night before. I knew this man well and agreed to go immediately.

What he failed to tell me, however, was that he had already called the sheriff's office and said that he was coming with a gun to shoot everyone and free his son! When I walked into the office, I faced four officers with guns drawn and ready to shoot! At first they thought I was the man who had called. After some explanation and apologies, I was taken to the prisoner. A lifetime of study and preparation for priesthood is required for such meetings. No matter what happens, the priest is like Christ, who said to the man being crucified with him, "Today yet, you will be with me in paradise."

Attendance at Holy Family continued to grow and many summer visitors joined us each year. Eventually, we had about 500 extra people at three Masses during summer weekends. It wasn't an easy Parish, but I enjoyed working with the children and taught them Czech carols. I also developed the choir and other church programs. After five years at Klacking Creek, I retired from the Priesthood and took residence in Lakewood Club, near Blue Lake.

CHAPTER 9

SPIRITUAL SON

In the late 1960's and early 1970's, the United States and many other countries were worried that South Vietnam would fall into the hands of Communists. I was also worried about this issue, but from a slightly different perspective. I had a Spiritual Son in Vietnam named Josef Thoai. This relationship came about when our diocesan mission office created a program whereby priests could sponsor a foreign seminarian for five years. The cost to the priest was $250.00 a year, which at the time was almost half of my annual income.

I thought about this program and decided to participate, as thanksgiving for the opportunity I'd been given to come to the United States. After spending two years in post-war refugee camps, I had found a good career and good fortune in America. Bishop Haas had sponsored me and I would pass the favor along. I sent a check and received a photograph of Josef, who was to study in Hong Kong. We corresponded regularly until late in the war, but at one point I lost track of him. When the war ended in 1975, I decided to go to Vietnam and find him. My trip was very interesting.

When the peace accord was reached, South Vietnam had a chance to become a strong nation. Nevertheless, the South Vietnamese people did not seem to like their government and silently opposed it. I felt that it was a sign of apathy on behalf of the people, to have a government and not actively participate in it. Especially when that government was supported by western democracies.

I stayed at Hotel Caravelle in Ho Chi Minh City, right next to the then empty parliament building. I inquired at the front desk as to the whereabouts of Father Josef Thoai. The main clerk had been a seminarian and offered to call the Jesuit Fathers in Saigon for information on Josef. Soon I was in a cab, headed toward an address where I was to supposed meet the Jesuits. I soon realized that the cab was taking me far outside the city. Finally, we pulled onto a dark, desolate cul-de-sac. It was about 9 o'clock at night and I was uneasy to be alone in this foreign place.

At the far end of the cul-de-sac was a gate guarded by Vietnamese soldiers. I cautiously approached one soldier and when he could finally see me he yelled, "Yankee go home!" At least he spoke some English! I turned on my heel and by chance noticed a cleric who was taking out some garbage. I went over to the house, rang the bell and viola. I was in the right place.

As the cab waited, the Jesuit cleric phoned Josef. He was living about 500 miles away in the city of Nha Trang. I told Josef that I would fly there the next day to see him, if he could pick me up at the airport. Returning to Saigon that night, I wondered about the risk of flying on the Vietnamese airline.

The next day, while waiting for my delayed flight, I met some interesting people at the airport. One man was an Italian on his way to visit the Bishop Dr. Diem, nephew of the late president Diem. Ngo Dihn Diem was called, "The Winston Churchill of Asia."

VIETNAM WAR STORIES

I met several Americans at the airport. Everyone had something to say about the war. One American worked for a company that produced military airplanes. He told me how a fleet of airplanes had been sold to a particular country, which intended to use them to bomb their enemy. At the request of the U.S. government, these planes had been outfitted so they would not have enough fuel to return from a key bombing mission.

Another man told me about American secret missions to assassinate key political and military leaders. The most disturbing stories were about how some American servicemen took advantage of the poor and unfortunate Vietnamese people. It was very hard for me to listen to these stories. To my mind, the Vietnam War was very different from the war I had lived through in Europe.

MISSING MY SON

My trip to Nha Trang started off on the wrong foot. It was very hot in Vietnam, so I left my luggage at Hotel Caravelle and traveled in a shirt without my collar. I was happy to learn that I was flying on an American-made airplane with American pilots. When I arrived at the airport in Nha Trang, I looked all over for Josef and could not find him. I later learned that he had been there with a jeep and a driver, but was wearing a Navy chaplain's uniform. We probably had not recognized each other.

Feeling a little stranded, I took a bus into the city. I walked to a cathedral-like church, which was high upon a hill overlooking the city. The doors of the church were locked and no one answered. From this hill, I could see a cross on a building several streets away. When I arrived at that building, I could tell that it was a Catholic orphanage. A little girl answered the door and luckily, she spoke English. I asked her if I might speak to a Nun.

After a few minutes, a tiny little Nun peaked around the door. I asked if she knew of Father Thoai? "Of course," she replied. She said that he could be found at the Bishop's compound. She called to another Sister and together they mounted a scooter, riding as the American's say, "sidesaddle." I followed behind in a rickshaw. The rickshaw man was so skinny and looked so hungry, that I felt bad being pulled by him. He had a hard time keeping the scooter Sisters in sight. I thought several times of stopping him and changing places so he could rest. How was I to talk to him, in Latin, German, Czech, English? All the while, my friend wondered and waited for me. Finally, after many years we met face to face.

The Bishop's compound contained several buildings. One was the residence of the Most Reverend Bishop. There was also a long dormitory building that housed a small seminary of which Josef was the Rector. During our meeting, Josef said the Bishop was preparing to attend a conference in Saigon, but would like to meet me before leaving the compound.

The Bishop was very cordial and we spoke for about 30 minutes. He gave Father Thoai permission to visit me in the United States, where I would teach him administration and finance. The Bishop was pleased with this offer, as he wanted Father Thoai to become his First Assistant. He also gave Father Thoai permission to fly back to Saigon with me, where we would have time to learn more about one another.

Later that evening, Father Thoai took me to a Parish where they were having a program. This was an experience very dear to me, because it reminded me so much of the programs we'd had in Czechoslovakia. It was different in that they had strobe lights and a good jazz band on stage. In this, I saw French influence.

In the 1800's the French supported many Christian missionaries in Vietnam, who taught hundreds of thousands of Vietnamese people about Jesus. Some French culture had taken hold and I noticed it in the people. After such an eventful day, I fell fast asleep on an impossibly hard bed in the seminary.

My stay in Vietnam opened my eyes to many things. With the American withdrawal, South Vietnam had to stand on its own. During most of 1974 and 1975, there was relative peace in South Vietnam. I found the Vietnamese people to be peaceful and freedom loving. After so many years of war, they were eager to enjoy a time of peace. So busied by their daily lives and jobs, they seemed to have forgotten the danger lying to the North. I could see that this was a very dangerous attitude.

LESSONS OF OCCUPATION

My historical perspective led me to notice an interesting trait in the South Vietnamese people. Both South Vietnam and Germany had been occupied by the United States. The Germans noticed what was good in the culture of the occupying nation and adopted it into their daily lives. The Vietnamese were very different. They seemed to adopt only the bad cultural tendencies of their occupiers.

91

Perhaps this was due of the extreme poverty in their country. I could see that everything the Americans left behind was completely looted by the Vietnamese. Buildings were stripped of every last door and window right down to the wiring, plumbing and utilities. Every nail and bolt was stripped away. These buildings could have been of great use to the community, but were left in ruin. I still don't understand this.

I also noticed that members of the South Vietnamese military, which Josef belonged to, lived with their entire family in the military barracks. One poor soldier, whose job it was to guard the bridge on Highway 1, lived with his entire family under the bridge. He had several small children. I felt fortunate to be an American.

LOSING MY SON

On our last day together, Josef took me on a tour of the beautiful Vietnamese countryside and introduced me to many people in traditional dress. At one point we stopped and looked north across the hills and forests, where the Viet Cong were watching and waiting. Perhaps my experiences in Europe had given me a sense for war. I could feel that the time was drawing near, but I could not tell Josef.

Soon after my return to the United States, events in South Vietnam took a turn for the worse. Josef changed his mind and decided to go to Rome, instead of coming to America. I telephoned him in Rome and told him that the North Vietnamese had surrounded Saigon. I begged him to come to the U.S.. He said, "Father, I am taking the last plane to Saigon tomorrow, because I have to be with my people." I understood exactly what he meant. I was disappointed, but filled with pride and respect for Josef.

Shortly after arriving in Saigon, Josef was placed in a "Re-Education Camp." I never heard from him again, but I tried to help him. I sent support through secret channels, which I cannot reveal here. I can only hope that he received my help and is alive today. All of my attempts to find him or to learn of his fate have failed.

Playing piano age 85.

Bishop Karel Otcenasek and myself in Hornì Jelenì.

Conductors and friends from the Czech Music Camp for Youth

CHAPTER 10

GRATITUDE

After the tragic story of my Spiritual Son, I shall tell this humorous story and resolve on a positive note. I was not yet a citizen of the United States, but had my Green card, when I traveled to San Diego 50 years ago. Being so close to Mexico, I decided to take a bus tour to Iguana. As we approached the Mexican border, the driver stopped the bus and asked, "Is everyone a US citizen?" The whole bus shouted, "Yes!" I shouted from the back seat, "No!"

A great silence fell over the bus. The driver looked back at me and asked, "Where are you from, sir?" I answered truthfully and loudly, "I am from Michigan." Everyone began laughing and the driver said, "Look at that smart guy, he is from Michigan!" He thought I was joking and so did everyone else. During the rest of the tour he addressed the Americans then added, "and the guy from Michigan." I came back to the United States elated that I was a citizen of Michigan!

I have enjoyed life in America. For 55 years, I've led my life with the American people. I've supported them through sickness and health, joy and sorrow, and war and peace. My life has made many interesting turns, but always with the quiet blessings of God.

I celebrated my 55th birthday on the Arctic Circle in Rovani-emi, Finland. My 80th birthday demanded something very special, so I celebrated at the music camp I founded in Horní Jelení. I invited all of my surviving classmates and about 40 relatives. Many old friends came to celebrate. It was one of the very best days of my life.

In this writing I have told my story. For this privilege, I am thankful. So many stories from my place in time have been lost to the ages. In conclusion, I want to tell the world that I thank God and all of the people of the United States, for giving me friendship, help and hope in my time of need. God Bless America!